CHAMPION
LANCASTRIANS

Elizabeth Ashworth

101088957

Published by Sigma Leisure – an imprint of
Sigma Press, 5 Alton Road, Wilmslow, Cheshire SK9 5DY, England.

British Library Cataloguing in Publication Data
A CIP record for this book is available from the British Library.

ISBN: 1-85058-833-3

Typesetting and Design by: Sigma Press, Wilmslow, Cheshire.

Cover photographs, left to right, top to bottom: Fred Dibnah; sundial on Towneley Hall; Eric Morecambe; Kathleen Ferrier; Joseph Livesey; Sir Henry Tate; Lifeboat memorial at St Annes; Robert Peel; St Michael's Church, Much Hoole

Printed by: Bell & Bain Ltd, Glasgow

Preface

Until around 1180 there was no such place as Lancashire. After the Norman Conquest of 1066, this area of the north was part of Yorkshire, and after his successful invasion, William the Conqueror gave away parcels of land to the Norman barons who had fought with him.

One of William's loyal supporters and cousin, Roger de Poitou, was rewarded by the king for his loyalty with the gift of land in the north. It was a lawless area, often invaded by the Scots and Roger built a stone castle at Lancaster, both as a residence and as a fortification against any further invasion from the north.

Around 1090, William the Conqueror's son, William Rufus, added land which is now in the south of Cumbria. But in 1102, Roger de Poitou joined his brother and other nobles in an unsuccessful rebellion against William's third son, Henry I, whom they didn't want to become king. The rebellion failed and his lands were confiscated and passed back into the ownership of the Crown. They were then given out again to those nobles who had supported Henry.

The Blackburn Hundred, for example, came into the possession of Robert de Lacy, who was the son of Ilbert de Lacy, who already owned land around Pontefract in Yorkshire and had built a castle there.

There are still many traces of the de Lacy family in the county. Robert de Lacy built Clitheroe Castle to protect his administrative estates and was responsible for other buildings including the ancient church of St Bartholomew at Colne. He also erected a Market Cross in Blackburn, at the top of Church Street, though it was later destroyed in the Civil War and never replaced.

The purple lions on Clitheroe's coat of arms are taken from the arms of the de Lacy family and it was from them that the town received its charter to hold a market. The stork on the top of Burnley's coat of arms rests one foot on a purple knot, another badge of the de Lacy family. And in both Clitheroe and Whalley you will find pubs called the De Lacy Arms.

Around 1180 there is evidence of Lancashire being first named as a county. Since then the area has been the birthplace of many notable people.

Writing this book about Champion Lancastrians posed not so much the problem of who to include, but who to leave out. During my research I was amazed by the number of talented people who, over hundreds of years, have achieved so much, not only for their county, but also for their country.

Some were born in Lancashire, died in Lancashire and lived here all their lives. Others were born here and moved away to achieve their fame and fortunes elsewhere, such as Frances Hodgson Burnett, the author of the well known children's novel *The Secret Garden*, who was born in Manchester. And I've also taken the liberty of including some, such as Kitty Wilkinson, who were born in another place but lived here for most of their lives and did so much for Lancashire that they cannot be disregarded.

Although there must have been others who lived in this area and achieved much during pre-historic, Saxon and Roman times, I've begun my record of *Champion Lancastrians* with the birth of the county in the twelfth century. From Robert de Lacy, parts of whose Norman buildings still remain, through John of Gaunt, the first hereditary Duke of Lancaster, to those who are still making their mark on the county to the present day, in the reign of our present Queen, the Duke of Lancaster, there are many scientists, inventors, artists and social reformers for whom we have cause to be grateful.

Although this list is far from exhaustive, I hope you find stories from my selection that will both interest and inspire you. Enjoy reading about these *Champion Lancastrians* – and may there be many more to come.

Elizabeth Ashworth

Contents

John of Gaunt

1340-1399

Duke of Lancaster

John of Gaunt was the fourth son of Edward III and Queen Philippa. He was born in Ghent in Flanders, in 1340, and, as it was traditional at that time to name princes after their birthplace, he was known as John of Ghent, which became corrupted into John of Gaunt.

His birth took place during a lull in the Hundred Years War, the long conflict between England and France, though because his mother was living in Ghent whilst the king was absent from England there were those who questioned his parentage.

It seems that he was brought up under the care of Henry, Duke of Lancaster. Henry was John's third cousin and both men were descended from Henry III, who had reclaimed the land that had become Lancashire from the rebellious Norman barons. John fought with Henry in France from the age of fifteen and at nineteen he married Blanche, the Duke's younger daughter.

After Henry's death two years later, John, because of his marriage, inherited half of his estates, and within the year, after the death of his wife's sister Maud from the plague, he became Duke of Lancaster and lived at Lancaster Castle. They had a son, Henry Bolingbroke, who was born at Bolingbroke Castle.

During this time Lancashire was made a County Palatine, which meant that the Duke had royal powers and could do things that were the privilege of a monarch, for example the courts of law were

Lancaster Castle, home of John of Gaunt

within his jurisdiction and he could appoint Sheriffs, Justices of the Peace and Judges.

John of Gaunt's eldest brother was the Black Prince and the two fought together in Spain and France – and it was whilst he was away that his wife Blanche also died of the Black Death. The plague was rampant at this time with outbreaks in 1348-9, 1361-2 and 1369.

John of Gaunt later married Constance of Castile in a political alliance. After her death he married Catherine Swynford, his mistress and mother to four of his children.

The Black Prince died a year before his father, Edward III, of an illness he had contracted in Spain. After the death of Edward III in 1377, the new heir to the throne was his young grandson, Richard of Bordeaux, but people feared that John of Gaunt would try to snatch the throne for himself. He was unpopular in the country because of his failures whilst fighting in France, particularly an incident in 1373, when many of his men died in the mountains of Auvergne.

A story began to circulate that his mother, Queen Philippa, made a confession on her deathbed that he was not her real son. It was said that she had given birth to a girl who had died when she accidentally lay on the baby in bed, and so as not to disappoint the king the dead baby had been substituted with the son of a Flemish woman. However John of Gaunt was appointed as protector of his young nephew, Richard II, and, although not king, he governed the country until Richard came of age.

When John of Gaunt died in 1399, Richard II seized the Duchy of Lancaster and banished John's son Henry Bolingbroke. But because of Richard's misrule he was brought to London and made to surrender the crown. Henry was made king in his place and became Henry IV. But not everyone in the family or in the country approved and there was a split between those who supported the Lancastrian king and those who became known as Yorkists. And the country was plunged into the civil war that was to become known as the Wars of the Roses. However, the Lancastrians were eventually triumphant and the Duchy of Lancaster remains the property of the monarch to this day.

John of Gaunt was buried alongside Blanche in a tomb in the old St Paul's Cathedral that was destroyed in the Great Fire of London, in 1666.

Humphrey Chetham

1580-1653

His generosity founded the first Public Library in Manchester

Humphrey Chetham was descended from a Norman family who took their name from the village of Chetham, now a suburb of Manchester. And because of his generosity the name is now immortalised by Chetham's School of Music and Chetham's Library in Manchester.

The son of a prosperous merchant, Humphrey Chetham was

Humphrey Chetham *(photograph courtesy of Chetham's Library)*

educated at Bishop Oldham's grammar school. At seventeen he was apprenticed to a linen draper named Samuel Tipping and after he had served his apprenticeship he began a business with his brother George, who was a grocer in London. They bought and imported yarn to be processed in Manchester and sold in London. They quickly became rich and successful and Humphrey was not only a businessman, but also acted as a banker, advancing loans to other traders. However he never took advantage and gained a reputation for honesty and integrity.

With his good business sense and money lending he quickly amassed a huge fortune and bought Clayton Hall in 1620 and Turton Tower, near Bolton in 1628.

But it was his prosperity that brought Humphrey to the notice of the king, Charles I. Charles needed money to pay his debts and one way he could do this was to sell knighthoods and other honours.

Consequently, middle class businessmen tried to avoid this 'honour' whenever they could and, as the scheme wasn't raising much income, the king decided that if a knighthood was offered and refused then a fine would have to be paid.

Humphrey Chetham, who was in fact a Parliamentarian, was offered a knighthood in 1631, but declined and paid his fine of £40. But four years later he was pressured into accepting the role of High Sheriff of Lancashire and then High Collector of Subsidies and Taxes for the County of Lancashire. One of his first tasks was to levy the tax of ship-money – an unpopular tax on coastal towns for the upkeep of the navy to offset the expenses of wars with France and Spain.

By 1643 he had been made General Treasurer of the County, despite trying to reject the role on the grounds of his ill health. It was a job that cost him a considerable amount of money because of bad debts, which he was obliged to pay himself. He also got into trouble over his coat of arms, supposedly choosing one to which he wasn't entitled – and he ended up paying a fine for that as well.

An honest, unassuming and diligent man, Humphrey Chetham was one of the first examples of a philanthropist, who set aside money from his wealth to provide benefits for others. During his life-time he paid for the upbringing and education of fourteen poor boys from Manchester, six from Salford and two from Droylsden, boarding them with other deserving families who would welcome the extra money. He kept a notebook in which he recorded his payments.

On his death on 12 October 1653, at the age of seventy-three, he left £7,000 to create and maintain a 'hospital', though this was a boarding school, or orphanage, rather than a place where the sick would go. The school would take forty boys and keep and educate them, though he stipulated that these boys should be the sons of honest and industrious parents, not beggars or rogues and that none should be illegitimate, lame or diseased. The boys stayed from the age of six until fourteen, when they were apprenticed to a trade. The school was also known as the Bluecoat School because of the seventeenth century uniform of blue frock coats, buckled shoes, yellow stockings and pancake hats.

Just before his death he had managed to buy the buildings where the school and library were to be housed for £400. They had originally been built as a residence for members of the clergy of what was then the Parish Church of Manchester, but had become the home of the Earl of Derby after the dissolution of the monasteries in the reign

Chetham Boys in 1894 *(photograph courtesy of Chetham's Library)*

on Henry VIII. But the buildings had become damaged during the Civil War and the purchase probably saved them from demolition.

He also gave £200 for the purchase of 'godly books, such as Calvin's, Preston's and Perkin's works, comments, or annotations on the Bible' or other books that the executors of his will should 'think most proper for the edification of the common people'. These books were to be 'chained up on desks, or to be fixed to the pillars, or in other convenient places in the parish churches of Manchester and Bolton-le-Moors, and in the chapels of Turton, Walmsley and Gorton'.

But maybe his most lasting gift was the money he left for the first public library in Manchester, the oldest in the English speaking world, for the use of scholars, as well as a fund of money to add to the collection of books over the years. Chetham's Library is still one of nation's most valuable antiquarian libraries and is open to the public by appointment. It houses more than 130,000 volumes of printed books, of which 60,000 were published before 1851.

Chetham's Hospital is now Chetham's School of Music. Established in 1969, it educates gifted young musicians from all over the north west; still retaining the principle of admitting pupils on merit, none is denied a place because of financial hardship. The school is still well funded and maintains poorer pupils.

So next time you're in Manchester and you walk past the Cathedral and Chetham's School of Music and Chetham's Library – all buildings that survived not only the Second World War but the IRA bomb of 1996 – spare a thought for Humphrey Chetham and his generosity. He is commemorated by a statue and a window in Manchester Cathedral and another statue and a mural in Manchester Town Hall.

Jonas Moore

1617-1679

Mathematician and Scientist

Jonas Moore was born on 8 February 1617 in the tiny hamlet of White Lee, near Higham, in the shadow of Pendle Hill. Even as a child he showed promise as a mathematician and was given help and encouragement by Christopher Towneley, whose nephew Richard Towneley was also to later collaborate with Jonas.

They became collectively known as the Towneley Group of scientists and they were responsible for rescuing the papers of Jeremiah Horrocks after the death of his friend William Crabtree.

Jonas Moore went to London to teach mathematics and in 1650 he published a mathematics textbook, *Arithmetic*.

Jonas worked on the project to drain the Fens in Norfolk, which resulted in the Bedford Level. He observed that when the sea came up the beach it did not do so in a straight line, so he built banks against the sea that corresponded with the tide line. He wrote an account of his work, which was published in 1685 after his death. It was his work here as a surveyor that boosted his reputation. He also worked to reclaim wasteland off the coast of Sussex and supervised the building of a mole, or sea wall, at Tangier. He also helped in the survey of London after the Great Fire in 1666.

According to John Aubrey (1626-1695), who wrote a collection of *Brief Lives*: 'He was tall and very fat, thin skin, fair, clear grey eye.' Aubrey also records that he worked for Oliver Cromwell during the Civil War and 'he made a model of a citadel for Oliver Cromwell, to bridle the City of London'.

But Jonas Moore was a royalist and after the restoration of the monarchy he was knighted in 1669, by Charles II and became Sir Jonas Moore. He was appointed Surveyor-General of the Ordnance. He also became a member of the Royal Society in 1674 and frequently spoke at meetings, though on one occasion he told the story about an experiment that had taken place in Lancashire, which involved a Mr Gascoigne teaching an Irish boy to fly. Apparently the boy flew over a river, but the shouts of the crowd frightened him and he fell and broke his legs. Whether he really believed that man could fly is not clear.

He was also a patron of the new Royal Observatory at Greenwich,

and the young John Flamsteed, who was to become the first Astronomer Royal, was his guest and benefited from his patronage. It was
whilst they were working at Greenwich that Jonas Moore and his
contemporaries in London worked with the observations made by
Richard Towneley in Burnley. It was during this time that scientists
were striving to find a way of discovering how to plot latitudes and,
together with the diary writer, Samuel Pepys, Jonas Moore founded
the Royal Mathematical School within Christ's Hospital. It aimed to
train boys in navigation techniques, so that they could serve the King
at sea.

Having been born on Pendle, there is an interesting link between
Jonas Moore and the Pendle Witches. In 1674, John Webster from
Clitheroe wrote a book called *The Displaying of Supposed Witchcraft*,
which was an attack on people's belief in witchcraft. At the time it
was necessary to gain permission to publish a book and this one came
before the Royal Society, where Jonas Moore was the person responsible for granting permission for its publication. But what makes it
more interesting is that Jonas' father, John Moore, was one of the
people who had accused Anne Whittle, known as Chattox, of witchcraft, claiming that she had bewitched his ale and made figures to cast
a spell on his son, Jonas' brother, who died in 1610. This evidence
helped to convict Anne Whittle and send her to her death on the
gallows at Lancaster. Perhaps Jonas Moore's sanctioning of this book
proved that he was more enlightened than his father was and that the
scientific discoveries of the time were helping to move society
forwards towards fact rather than superstition.

He became ill with a fever after returning to London from a visit to
Portsmouth and he died on 27 August 1679. At his funeral, sixty
salutes were fired. He was buried at the Tower of London.

Jeremiah Horrocks

1619-1641

First person to observe the Transit of Venus

Jeremiah Horrocks would almost certainly have been better known as an astronomer if he had lived longer. But despite his early death, at the age of only twenty-two, he made astronomical history on 24 November 1639 by being the first person to predict and observe the Transit of Venus across the face of the sun.

His family home was at Toxteth, at that time a small hamlet near Liverpool, and his father was James Horrocks, a watchmaker – which at that time was a scientific profession.

Jeremiah Horrocks, registered as Horrox, entered Emmanuel College, Cambridge as a sizar on 11 May 1632 at the age of fourteen, which was not unusual for those times. A sizar was a poor student who probably could not afford to pay fees, but might earn his keep and gain his education by performing chores – a way of obtaining a degree and, hopefully, an appointment as a minister.

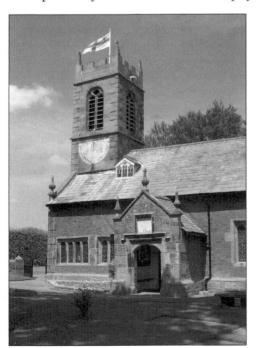

St Michael's, Much Hoole where Jeremiah Horrocks was a curate

But although he was fascinated by astronomy there was no such course taught in Britain and Jeremiah's studies would probably have consisted mostly of Latin and theology. Astronomy was taught in some of the continental universities, but as he had no hope of studying there, Jeremiah resolved to educate himself in the subject with the help of all the books he could find.

In a letter to his friend, William Crabtree, he says: "I was much pained not to have anyone to whom I could look for guidance, or indeed for the sympathy of companionship in my endeavours ..."

Horrocks also worked on his lunar theory – eventually showing that the moon's orbit was elliptical. He also commenced a series of observations on the tides and was interested in comets too and concluded that they "move in an elliptical figure or near to it". He wrote to William Crabtree about all this, but no papers survive relating to his observations or theories.

In June 1639 Jeremiah Horrocks moved to Hoole, near Preston, where it is believed that he was the curate at the church of St Michael, though some historians believe that he was a tutor to the children of John Stones at Carr House, who was a benefactor of the church. This may be true because he did live at Carr House and his observations were made from there, through the small window above the front door.

The astronomer Kepler had predicted a transit of Venus in 1631, though this wasn't visible from Europe. After having studied Kepler's calculations Horrocks realised that the transit always occurs twice, with an eight-year gap. There had been a transit in 1631 and so the next was due that same year, 1639. It would occur again in 1761/69, then 1874/82 and more recently we saw it in 2004 and it will occur again in 2012. It was Horrocks' prediction that a transit of Venus would occur in 1769, but would only be visible on the other side of the world, that was one reason for Captain Cook's scientific expedition to Tahiti.

In his work *Venus in Sole Visa* (Venus on the face of the Sun, which was published in 1662 after his death) Horrocks says: "I watched carefully on the 24th from sunrise to nine o'clock, and from a little before ten until noon, and at one in the afternoon, being called away in the intervals by business of the highest importance which, for these ornamental pursuits, I could not with propriety neglect." Though he doesn't comment on what his exact duties were.

Understanding the dangers of looking directly into the sun, Horrocks made calculations and traced a circle on some paper and watched as the shadow of Venus moved across the sun.

Jeremiah Horrocks went on to write: "About fifteen minutes past three in the afternoon, when I was again at liberty to continue my labours, the clouds, as if by divine interposition, were entirely dispersed, and I was once more invited to the grateful task of repeating my observations. I then beheld a most agreeable spectacle, the object of my sanguine wishes, a spot of unusual magnitude and of a perfectly circular shape, which had already fully centred upon the sun's disc on the left, so that the limbs of the Sun and Venus precisely coincided, forming an angle of contact. Not doubting that this was really the shadow of the planet, I immediately applied myself sedulously to observe it."

Horrocks could only watch for around another thirty minutes though because then the sun set, but it was long enough for him to make his observations and calculations which are recorded in his book.

In 1874, after much lobbying, a memorial was mounted in Westminster Abbey opposite that to Newton. It reads: "In memory of Jeremiah Horrocks, Curate of Hoole in Lancashire who died on 3rd of Jan, 1641 in or near his 22nd year."

There is also a memorial plaque and a stained glass window in the church at Much Hoole. Jeremiah Horrocks also has a crater on the moon named after him.

Richard Towneley

1629-1707

First Weatherman

When Charles Towneley died fighting for the king at the Battle of Marston Moor in 1644, his eldest son Richard Towneley inherited his estate at Burnley.

In the family tradition, Richard was a scientist and he ran some experiments at Towneley Hall that assisted the Astronomer Royal, John Flamsteed. The Towneley Time Trials of 1675 plotted the course of the sun at noon each day throughout one year in relation to a meridian line. It helped to show that Christian Huygens had been correct in saying that not every day was exactly twenty-four hours long, but that over a year each day averaged twenty-four hours. After a claim by Juan Cruzado, the chief navigator of Spain, that this was untrue, Flamsteed had prepared his own table called the *Equation of Natural Days* and it was this that he asked Richard Towneley to check for him.

The trials clearly showed that the days around September were shorter than the ones around November, but that the earth did rotate at a constant speed throughout the year.

This work led to the creation of Greenwich Mean Time and Richard Towneley also worked with the scientists at Greenwich on the accurate measurement of time by a reliable clock, which would in turn allow the plotting of longitude that was so vital to the navigation of the seas.

He helped to design the two Great Clocks, one of which is now in the British Museum, which were then the most accurate in the world. On 6 July 1676 John Flamsteed wrote to him to say: 'We shall have a pair of watch clocks down here tomorrow, with pendulums of 13 foot and pallets partly after your manner, with which I hope we may try these experiments much more accurately...'

John Flamsteed also travelled north to stay at Towneley Hall in Burnley to study the astronomical papers of Lancashire scientists such as Horrocks, Crabtree and Gascoigne, which the Towneley Group had rescued.

Richard Towneley was also very interested in the weather and is sometimes called 'the first weatherman' as he was the first person to keep regular records of rainfall and other weather conditions. He

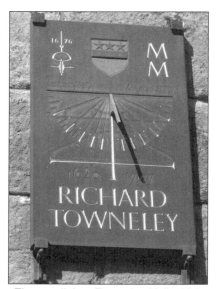

The sundial on Towneley Hall which commemorates Richard Towneley

began his experiments in 1677 and made records three times a day for a total of twenty-six years. He designed a gauge that collected rain in a twelve-inch cylinder and fixed it to the roof of Towneley Hall. Rather than making measurements each day he kept a record of the running total to avoid multiplying small errors. He also recorded wind speed and direction, and air pressure.

He was in regular correspondence with members of the Royal Society and worked with Henry Power from Halifax on experiments into the relationship between air pressure and volume, which was later to become known as Boyle's Law. The two men put equal volumes of air and mercury into U-shaped tubes that were sealed at one end, an early version of the barometer, and recorded the expansion of the air at different heights on Pendle Hill. They demonstrated that air at the top of the hill reduced in volume as the tube was carried down and vice versa. They also took these instruments down local lead mines to make measurements underground.

It was whilst he was in London, delivering a package for his friend Henry Power, that he was invited to a meeting of the Royal Society, where he discussed his hypothesis with Robert Boyle, leading Boyle to formulate his law. The two men remained friends and regularly corresponded with each other.

Richard Towneley also improved the micrometer, which was used for astronomical observations and introduced the instrument to John Flamsteed.

Although Richard Towneley was an eminent scientist of his generation his name is not as well-known as others, because the family were Roman Catholics and so did not merit public acknowledgement of their work. Now though, the work of Richard Towneley is more widely recognised and a sundial has been added to the south wall of Towneley Hall in recognition of his achievements.

Robert Gillow

1704-1772

Founder of the famous furniture company

Born in Singleton in 1704, Robert Gillow was the founder of the Gillow furniture making company. At the time Lancaster, where he was based, was a major port with ships from the West Indies arriving laden with rum and sugar. When the ships docked with their cargoes packed into wooden crates, Robert Gillow, who had previously worked as a ship's carpenter and sailed to the West Indies, saw an opportunity to use the timber in his small cabinet making business. It was his use of mahogany that was a turning point which transformed his small enterprise into the famous furniture manufacturer Gillows, and his work is still admired and collected as valuable antique pieces to this day.

He produced tables and chairs, clock cases and other items of furniture that sold well, not only in the local area, but also as exports, often packed with shoes and hats, to plantation owners in the West Indies.

He became a freeman of Lancaster in 1728 and married Agnes Fell in 1730. They had two sons, Richard and Robert. Richard, born in 1734, studied architecture before returning to Lancaster. Several important Lancaster buildings were designed by him, including the Custom House on St George's Quay, which is now the Maritime Museum. Robert, born in 1745, managed the London showrooms which were opened on Oxford Street in 1769, the firm having had a London warehouse for some years previously. Later they also made billiard tables, as the game became very popular in the late 18th century, using slate from Cumbrian mines.

The opening of the London branch brought the firm wider recognition and although there were transport costs, the manufacturing continued in Lancaster as rates of pay for the workers were cheaper. Though some final assembly of furniture took place in London.

The firm also employed travelling salesmen with illustrated pattern books, to promote their products.

The firm was known for producing conventional, unfussy furniture that would appeal to the newly wealthy middle classes in Manchester and Liverpool. They concentrated on solid well made furniture, avoiding anything that was too fashionable, and became

The Judges' Lodgings in Lancaster where you can find the Gillow Museum

known for quality and value for money. Carvings were kept to a minimum, but painted furniture that would blend with soft furnishings and wallpaper was popular during the late 18th century. And in 1785 Gillows also began to make upholstery.

The company later expanded into fitting out luxury yachts and ocean going liners. The Royal Yacht *Victoria and Albert*, Tsar Alexander III's yacht *Livadia* and the ships *Lusitania*, *Heliopolis* and *Cairo* were all fitted out by Gillows.

The firm later merged with Warings of Liverpool to form Waring and Gillow, following collaboration for the 1900 Paris Exhibition Pavilion contract, and their final ship-fitting contract was for the Cunard liner *Queen Elizabeth*.

There is a Gillow museum in Lancaster and examples of Robert Gillow's work can be found around Lancashire at Lancaster City Museum, Lancaster Town Hall, and Leighton Hall, which was the home of his grandson.

John Kay

1704-1780

His invention transformed handloom weaving

Handloom weaving was a common trade in Lancashire. Most of the farmers who reared sheep used the wool from their flocks for cloth and the wool was spun and woven in the farmhouse by members of the family. Cloth is produced by weaving one thread alternately under and over threads strung onto a loom. The warp thread is attached to the loom at the top and the bottom on heald frames and a mechanism, originally worked by foot, raises and lowers the frames so that the weft thread, attached to a shuttle, can be passed backwards and forwards to form the cloth.

John Kay © *Blackburn with Darwen Library and Information Services*

The women and children spun the thread and the men would weave – partly because it was a fairly strenuous job that involved not only raising and lowering the heald frames but throwing the shuttle from one side of the loom to the other by hand.

However, John Kay found a way to mechanise the process of sending the shuttle backwards and forwards. This innovation began the move from home based handloom weaving, to thousands of people producing cloth in factories all over Lancashire during the Industrial Revolution.

John Kay was born at the hamlet of Park, just outside Bury, on the 17 June 1704, though his father had died before his birth. When he grew up he was apprenticed to a reedmaker – a man who made the comb-like attachment to the loom which kept the warp threads apart and was pulled down against the weft threads to compact the cloth. As the name suggests, these were originally made from reeds, but John Kay soon designed a device made from polished wire instead, and he worked selling and fitting them to looms all over the country. He also invented a machine for twisting and cording mohair and worsted.

But it is for his 'flying shuttle' that he is best remembered. It not only speeded up the weaving process but also meant that cloth wider than an arm's length could be produced

Many weavers quickly made use of the invention, but were reluctant to pay any royalties to John Kay for its use, even though he had patented the design in 1733. When his patent expired in 1747 he begged Parliament for legislation that would allow him to collect his dues, and when he failed he went to France. But he did little better there. The French weavers were reluctant to use the "navette volante", and although he was granted a payment of around £120 a year, he returned to Lancashire.

But the Luddites, who were determined to break any machinery that they believed would harm their own livelihoods were on his trail, and one night he had to run for his life across the moors near Bury with a murderous mob in pursuit. Consequently he returned to France and died there in poverty around 1780.

Kay Gardens in Bury has an impressive monument in memory of his achievements.

The memorial to John Kay in Kay Gardens at Bury

John Collier 'Tim Bobbin'

1708-1786

First author to write in Lancashire dialect

John Collier, known as Tim Bobbin, has been described as 'the Robert Burns of Lancashire' and was the first author to write in Lancashire dialect.

Tim was born at Urmston in 1708. He was the third son born into a family of nine children and his father was a curate and schoolmaster. It was common at this time for many clerical 'livings' or 'benefices' to be held by one rich man who enjoyed the income whilst paying a curate a miserly sum of money to do all the work. The Collier family was, consequently, very poor and writing about his own childhood, in a third person narrative, Tim Bobbin says: "In the reign of Queen Anne he was a boy and one of nine children of a poor curate in Lancashire, whose stipend never amounted to £30 a year, and consequently the family must feel the iron teeth of penury with a witness."

He records that he lived on "water porridge, buttermilk and jannock, till he was between thirteen and fourteen years of age, when Providence began to smile on him on his advancement to a pair of Dutch looms".

In fact his father had hoped that he would join the Church, but their poverty made that impossible and instead Tim Bobbin was apprenticed to a Dutch born weaver named Johnson in May 1722. However at the age of seventeen he made use of the education his father had given him and left the weaving trade to become a travelling schoolmaster, holding classes in Bury, Middleton, Oldham and Rochdale both during the day and in the evenings. The pay was very poor, but as he travelled around Tim Bobbin began to make notes about the various ways that language was used in different towns and villages.

He later accepted the position of assistant master at a free school at Milnrow, near Rochdale, for a salary of £10 a year. He writes, "I by divine Providence, vailing my skullcap to the mitres, in November 1727, commenced schoolmaster at Milnrow." This 'vailing my skullcap to the mitres' referred to his gaining a licence to teach from the Bishop, which he eventually received after teaching here for twelve years as an assistant master and three years as the master after succeeding Mr Pearson, who became ill with gout.

Tim Bobbin's grave in St Chad's parish churchyard at Rochdale

It was around this time that Tim Bobbin began to write prose and verse as well as developing his talent for sketching portraits and caricatures. He also taught himself to play the flute and was regarded as a very eligible bachelor by the ladies who lived locally.

However he married a girl from Yorkshire, Mary Clay, who had come to visit her aunt, Mrs Butterworth, at Milnrow. They were married on 1 April 1744, when Tim Bobbin was thirty-five years old and his bride was twenty-one, and settled in a house near the school. The garden overlooked the river and Tim Bobbin spent a lot of time there with his books and his flute and even his meals as his students came from the school next door to have their work marked. This leisurely approach to life, along with the drinking and feasting at various inns all around, seems to have been prompted by the £300 that his wife brought to the marriage. But soon the money was all gone and Tim Bobbin was forced to face reality and look for a way of earning some more.

He began painting altarpieces for country churches and sign-boards for inns and later toured around the inns selling caricatures to commercial travellers. He also wrote satires in both prose and verse and two years after his marriage he published *A View of the Lancashire Dialect*, sometimes known as *Tummas and Meary*, which is a comic dialogue between two characters – Thomas and Mary. Written in Lancashire dialect, with a glossary of the Lancashire words and phrases he had collected over the years, it made Tim Bobbin a household name throughout the county.

Five years after the publication he was offered the job of head clerk by a Mr Hill from Halifax and he set out with his wife and family for Yorkshire. But sitting at a desk all day long did not suit him and, although he was receiving a house rent-free and double the salary of that as a teacher, he wrote to a friend that he felt as if he had become a slave. Before a year was out, he had persuaded Mr Hill to cancel their agreement and returned to the house and school in Milnrow where his old job was still vacant.

Here he continued to supplement his income with his painting and writing, and though he was still fond of his drink, his wife Mary stood by him and they had six children. Tim Bobbin died in July 1786 at the age of seventy-seven just a few weeks after the death of Mary. They are both buried in the churchyard at St Chad's, Rochdale with this epitaph on their gravestone:

Here lies John with his Mary
cheek by jowl they never vary;
No wonder they do so agree,
John wants no punch and Moll no tea.

Some suppose that the verse was written by John Collier himself, though others think not. However, perhaps fittingly, there are now various public houses around the region named the Tim Bobbin.

James Hargreaves

1720-1777

The inventor of The Spinning Jenny

During the mid eighteenth century many weavers began to use John Kay's flying shuttle and though it aided the speed at which they could weave cloth they found that their wives and daughters were unable to spin enough thread to keep them supplied. So it became obvious that there was a need to mechanise the production of the spun thread in some way. Many inventors were working on ways to spin cotton more efficiently, including Thomas Highs of Leigh, but it is James Hargreaves from Stanhill, up on the hill above Oswaldtwistle, whom history remembers as the inventor of a spinning machine named the Spinning Jenny: the first machine that allowed more than one thread to be spun at the same time.

Although James Hargreaves never went to school and could neither read nor write, it is recorded that he had 'an interest in mechanics despite his lack of letters'. And although there were never any paintings made of him, he was described as 'a tall, well-built man with black hair'.

The Spinning Jenny had eight spindles bolted together and was powered by one large wheel. The spinning was powered by hand but the output was increased eight-fold. It was still small enough to fit into a kitchen and had the advantage that it was so easy to use even a child could spin on it – and many did. The main disadvantage was that the thread produced was rather coarse and tended to break more easily than hand spun thread and so it was only suitable for the weft thread (the thread carried by the shuttle, as opposed to the warp thread, which is strung to the loom).

There is a story that the machine got its name because his daughter was called Jenny, and one day she knocked over the family spinning wheel. As the wheel rotated on its own, Hargreaves was inspired to build a machine where one wheel simultaneously spun several threads. Contrary to what might be thought, he did not have a daughter named Jenny; the name is thought to come from 'gin' – an abbreviation of 'engine'.

James Hargreaves built his first machine in 1767 with the help of a pocket-knife and soon his relatives and friends were using one too. But the machine proved very unpopular with many textile workers who believed that its invention would take their jobs. The Luddites as these protestors came to be known, went around the county destroying every Spinning Jenny they could find. In 1768 rioters gathered at the market cross in Blackburn, at the top of Church Street, and marched to Stanhill where they smashed over twenty Jennies that James Hargreaves had built in a barn. It was more than he could bear and he moved away to Nottingham.

He continued to work on his invention and in 1770 tried to patent it, but by then so many other copies had been made that it was impossible for him to claim the invention as his own.

He died in Nottingham in 1777, by which time there were more than twenty thousand Jennies in regular use.

Richard Arkwright

1732-1792

Father of The Factory System

Richard Arkwright is remembered in Lancashire for his invention of the Water Frame, and it was because of his efforts to mechanise the production of cotton that the textile industry moved from cottages into factories, creating the wealth upon which many Lancashire towns were built. He has been called the 'Father of the Factory System' although his original trade was as a barber and wig maker.

Richard Arkwright was born in Preston on 23 December 1732, the thirteenth child of Thomas Arkwright. Although he never attended school, his cousin Ellen taught him to read and write and he was apprenticed to a barber called Nicholson in Kirkham before opening his own barber's shop in Bolton in around 1760. The site of his shop, now a newsagent's, has a plaque which marks it: "Sir Richard Arkwright inventor of the water frame for cotton spinning occupied a shop on this site as a barber and peruke (wig) maker from 1760 to 1768."

In 1755 he married Patience Holt of Bolton and they had a son, Richard, but Patience died only two years later. In 1761 he married Margaret Biggins of Leigh and they had a daughter, Susannah. His second wife had a small income, which he used to establish his wig-making business. He had formulated a method of dyeing human hair and spent much of his time travelling the country to buy hair from the girls at the hiring-fairs.

When the fashion for wigs went into a decline he decided to move into textiles. Around this time many

Richard Arkwright © *Blackburn with Darwen Library and Information Services*

inventions were being tried to mechanise the production of cotton spinning and weaving. James Hargreaves had invented the Spinning Jenny, which could spin cotton on up to eight spindles, but was still worked by hand. Richard Arkwright was interested in producing a machine that worked mechanically. With the help of John Kay – a clockmaker from Warrington, not the inventor of the flying shuttle – whom he paid to build a prototype, he worked on his Water Frame in a room he rented in Preston in the house of the headmaster of Preston Grammar School, now called Arkwright House. They worked here in secrecy, although some of the neighbours were alarmed by the strange noises and thought the house was haunted.

In 1769 he patented his invention after gaining financial backing from John Smalley, a publican and paint merchant of Preston. Needing a suitable site to test his water-powered invention he moved to Derbyshire and went into partnership with Jedediah Strutt. In 1776, at Cromford, in the valley of the River Derwent, where he located a fast and reliable stream that did not ice over in the wintertime, they built the world's first successful water-powered cotton spinning mill. It had the added advantage of being in a fairly secluded place and so was less accessible to the Luddites, who were intent on destroying any new machinery that they believed would cost them their livelihoods – though a mill of Arkwright's near Chorley, on the River Yarrow, was burned to the ground in 1779 and never rebuilt.

By 1775 he had patented another ten pieces of machinery, including devices for carding (straightening) the cotton to prepare it for spinning, which resulted in his factory being able to take cotton from the raw bales to finished cloth.

The machinery was relatively easy to operate and he employed an unskilled workforce, including children. By 1789 he was employing around 800 people at Cromford Mill and his profits were well on the way to making him very rich, though he also built housing and a chapel for his workers and their families, creating the first factory village.

Patents usually lasted for fourteen years, or longer if an extension was granted, but many people began to use Arkwright's invention without his authorisation. He gathered information about several firms and took a Colonel Mordaunt to court, but was not successful. In 1785 Richard Arkwright went to court again, at Westminster Hall before Mr Justice Buller and a special jury. But John Kay gave evidence against him, saying that he and a man named Thomas Highs of Leigh had originally worked on a spinning machine, but had run out of money. The insinuation was that Richard Arkwright had stolen the ideas for his machinery, rather than invented anything new. As a

Arkwright House, Preston

result of this his patents were rescinded. But he was already a very wealthy man. The following year he was knighted and then in 1787 appointed the High Sheriff of Derbyshire.

The lapsing of the patents also meant that other entrepreneurs could now legally use the new technology to produce cotton, and the Industrial Revolution began as factories were built all across the county of Lancashire. People who had previously lived in the countryside swarmed to towns like Preston, Blackburn, Bolton and Burnley to work in the mills.

Richard Arkwright died on 3 August 1792 and his obituary described him as being 'immensely rich' before ending by noting that 'His economy and frugality bordered very nearly on parsimony. He was, however, if not great, a very useful character."

Great? Useful? Or perhaps a bit of a rogue? Lancashire has something of a love/hate relationship with Richard Arkwright. There are those who claim that he used and manipulated people for his own gain, and that he was a cheat. And there are those who say that it was upon his work that the Lancashire textile industry was founded.

At the time of his death he had factories in Derbyshire, Staffordshire, Lancashire and Scotland, and his empire was worth over half a million pounds. So it's safe to say that, whatever your opinion of him, there's no doubt that he was very successful.

Francis Egerton, third Duke of Bridgewater

1736-1803

From broken heart to canal builder

Transport was very important to the growing prosperity of Lancashire during the Industrial Revolution. Along with the railways, canals were vital for the transportation of raw goods and finished products – and it was because of a broken heart that Francis Egerton turned to canal building and built the Bridgewater Canal, often referred to as England's first canal as it was the first to be built without following an existing watercourse.

Francis Egerton was born on 3 May 1736 and had an unhappy childhood. He was only nine years old when his father died of tuberculosis and his elder brother, John, became the second Duke of Bridgewater. Their mother remarried and had little or no interest in either of her sons – especially Francis, who was sickly and considered to be so intellectually inferior that there was talk of excluding him as a successor to the dukedom. But before any decision was reached his brother John also died, and at the age of twelve Francis became the third, and last, Duke of Bridgewater.

Everyone expected that he would soon die too and so no great effort was made to provide him with much of an education. However Francis grew older and as his health improved his guardians sent him on a Grand Tour of Europe, to broaden his learning and a scholar by the name of Wood was chosen to travel with him and tutor him.

Francis though showed little interest in the arts and after two years he returned to England and seemed mostly interested in horse racing and gambling – then he fell in love with Elizabeth Gunning.

Elizabeth and her sister Maria were the celebrities of the age. They had come to London in 1751 from Ireland and their beauty caused crowds to gather to try to catch a glimpse of them wherever they went. In fact it's recorded that the king, George II, ordered a file of guards to clear the path down the Mall for them to walk on Sunday afternoons.

Elizabeth married the Duke of Hamilton one night in a spontaneous midnight ceremony, but he didn't live long afterwards and she was a widow when Francis Egerton fell in love with her. She agreed to marry him, but he asked her to break off her relationship with her sister, now Lady Coventry, whose name was constantly linked to the scandals of the day. But Elizabeth refused to give up her sister and the engagement was ended. The following year her sister died, a victim of lead poisoning caused by the make-up she used to whiten her face, and in the meantime Elizabeth had married Colonel Jack Campbell, who later became the Duke of Argyll. The Duke of Bridgewater, although he threw a ball to show his indifference, afterwards withdrew from society and had nothing more to do with women. There were no women servants at either his house in London or his house at Worsley.

Instead, he turned his attention to running his estate, but soon realised that the main obstacle to prosperity in the region was lack of transport. The roads around Manchester were rutted tracks and although he had coal to sell from his mines in Worsley to ready markets in Manchester and Salford, there was no cost effective way to get it there.

Whilst travelling on the continent, although his tutor was disappointed at his lack of interest in the classics, Francis Egerton had been keenly interested in the canals he saw there, and so he decided that he would build a canal to transport his coal.

His idea was to construct a canal that would cross the River Irwell, with locks on both sides of the river, but James Brindley from Derbyshire, who had no formal education but had built a reputation for clever engineering, had a better idea. He suggested carrying the canal over the river on an aqueduct. Many scoffed at his suggestion, but the Duke had faith in him and building work began, with Francis Egerton funding all the expenses. The canal was eventually carried on high embankments and across the river on three sandstone arches. And when the canal leaked, Brindley invented a new mortar to keep it watertight.

At its beginning, the engineers tunnelled into the hill at Worsley to connect the coal mines directly to the canal, though it was John Gilbert, the Duke's land agent, who had proposed taking the canal right into the mine. As well as solving a drainage problem in the mine the water was used to supply the canal.

On 17 July 1761, two years after the work had begun, the first boat loaded with coal sailed from the mines at Worsley across the Irwell at Barton and into Castlefield in Manchester. Here, Brindley had built a waterwheel that hoisted five tons of coal an hour from the barges to street level, so that purchasers would not have to carry heavy loads to the top of the hill.

The Bridgewater Canal at Potato Wharf in Castlefield, Manchester

There is a story that records how the Duke used to enjoy travelling down the canal on one of the 'fly boats' that he provided for passenger traffic. He enjoyed watching the trading in coal and one day as he was standing on the wharf in Manchester, customarily dressed in his fairly shabby clothes, a man who had filled a sack of coal for his own household use called to him, "Hey! Mister! Gi' me a lift with this sack o' coal!" The Duke helped the man hoist the sack up onto his shoulder and carry it away, until someone who had witnessed the exchange ran to tell the man that it was the Duke himself he had asked for assistance. Horrified, the man turned to make his apologies, but the Duke was gone.

Following their success the Duke and Brindley decided to extend the canal westwards to link Manchester with the River Mersey and the port of Liverpool. However they struggled to get the venture started as many people thought that building a canal twenty-eight miles long across bogs, through tunnels and over rivers and valleys was impossible. Another problem was that the uneducated Brindley could not produce any convincing plans on paper as he could barely read and write and made his plans in his head – and when an engineering difficulty presented itself he would retire to his bed for a day or two to think it through. Once, when answering questions from a

Parliamentary committee he demonstrated his ideas for the Barton Aqueduct by making a model from a cheese.

But despite strenuous opposition Parliament granted permission for the building work, though the money still needed to be raised and the Duke found it difficult to raise funds as no-one wanted to invest in what they regarded as a folly.

It took five years and much scrimping, saving and borrowing of small sums of money before the Bridgewater Canal was completed as far as Runcorn. By 20 October 1771 the Duke's debt had risen to £133,219 whilst his yearly interest payments were £5,400 and the profits from the canal amounted to just £3,546. And because of a dispute over land just south of Warrington with Sir Richard Brooke, it wasn't until 21 March 1776 that the full length of the canal was opened. Then the profits increased and the country began to see the value of a canal system as a means of transport.

The canal halved the cost of coal in the city and when the steam engine came, Manchester had a ready supply of cheap coal to run its factories. The ease of importing and exporting goods along the canal to Liverpool also added to the growth and prosperity of both cities and Liverpool quickly became the chief port on the west coast of England.

It's strange to think that if the marriage of Francis Egerton and Elizabeth Gunning had gone ahead, a lack of cheap and easy transport might have meant that the towns of Lancashire would never have benefited from the same level of trade and industry that they did because of the canals. Francis Egerton may have had his heart broken, but the legacy that he left has lasted far longer than any love affair, and though nowadays the canals are no longer used as much for industrial transport, they are a source of much pleasure for leisure activities.

Charles Townley

1737-1805

Collector of works of art

Charles Townley was born at Towneley Hall on 1 October 1737 and is perhaps the best known of the family. He became an important collector of works of art and when he died in 1805 his entire collection was purchased for £20,000, through an Act of Parliament, to be displayed in the British Museum where it can still be seen.

Although Lancashire born from an old Lancashire family, Charles lived mostly in London, but did often stay at Towneley Hall, where there are many items that he bought.

In the entrance hall there is the Barcroft table bought in 1795; in the Red Regency Room, the Hayward fireplace he bought in 1780; in the Oak Room, off the Long Gallery is the Todmorden bed given to him by Thomas Dunham Whitaker around 1802; and the magnificent Flemish altarpiece in the chapel is also thought to have been installed by him, along with the Italian painting.

Outside, Charles Townley planted thousands of trees in the grounds of the hall to make a more picturesque view, including the large cedar of Lebanon near to where the war memorial now stands.

After the death of his father, in 1742 from smallpox, Charles inherited Towneley Hall when he was just five years old. At the age of ten, he was sent to France to study at the Catholic college in Douai, where he was three or four years younger than his classmates. In 1753, he left to be tutored privately by John Turberville Needham, before returning to Lancashire to take on his responsibilities.

It was Charles who, around 1762, dropped the extra 'e' from his surname and, although the hall continues to be called Towneley Hall, the family from this point were known simply as Townley.

In August 1767 he set off on his first Grand Tour, partly to buy works of art for the hall, which was in the process of being renovated. He visited Rome, arriving there on Christmas Day and bought artwork and marble sculptures in particular, spending a total of over £2,000.

He had intended the marbles for Towneley Hall, but decided that he would prefer to have a London house. He bought a house in Whitehall in 1769, but it proved too small to display his sculptures.

Meanwhile he undertook a second Italian Tour in October 1771.

Towneley Hall, the home of Richard Towneley and Charles Townley

His main aim was to visit Sicily, but he became ill in June 1772 and returned to Naples to rest. It was there, on 22 July that he purchased the marble bust of Clytie, which became his favourite piece.

On his return he sold the house in Whitehall and took temporary accommodation in Crown Street. He also made a third visit to Italy whilst waiting to move into a larger home on a new development on Park Street, overlooking St James's Park, where there was space to display his art collection – though in June 1780 he had to escape from the house by carriage, taking *Clytie* with him, after he was attacked by a mob during the Gordon Riots (a protest against the Catholic Relief Act).

It was in August 1781 that Johann Zoffany began his famous painting, which shows the library at Park Street. It depicts forty of the most important sculptures in Charles Townley's collection, though not all the sculptures were actually in the room as portrayed.

It was said that Charles Townley was a quiet and unassuming man not wishing to show off his wealth, but who bought the art and opened his house to people who wished to see it. The Prince of Wales visited to see the sculptures in 1786 and the house became a popular venue, with hundreds of people visiting each year. A catalogue was available to visitors which listed over 180 works of art.

St Peter's parish church at Burnley where Charles Townley is buried in the family vault

He did consider moving his sculpture gallery north to Towneley Hall, but thought that removing it from London would deny too many people the pleasure of seeing the works of art. However it was Charles Townley who invited J.M.W. Turner to Lancashire to produce illustrations for Whitaker's *History of Whalley*. It was also Charles Townley who bought the bronze Roman parade helmet that was discovered at Ribchester and can now be seen in the British Museum, although there is a replica in the museum at Ribchester.

He died at Park Street in 1805 and was buried in the family vault at St Peter's Church in Burnley.

John Taylor and George Taylor

1739-1802 and 1753-1804

From sick animals to humans:
The Whitworth Doctors

The Taylor family from the village of Whitworth, near Bacup, were in the business of healing for several generations, although it was the two brothers John Taylor and George Taylor whose fame spread countrywide.

Their father James Taylor had been a farrier and animal doctor, and although the two brothers still treated sick animals, it was their success in using their remedies to treat humans that built their reputation.

The better-known of the two doctors was John, although it was George, the younger brother, who was granted a licence, issued by the Bishop of Chester, to practise 'the Several Arts or professions of Physic and Chirurgery within and throughout the Diocese of Chester'.

The brothers practised medicine from their home, Whitworth House, near to Doctor's Wood where they gathered the herbs that they used to make their remedies. Their patients varied from the poor people who lived locally, or came to lodgings on the outskirts of the village, to rich gentry who travelled the length of the country and stayed, sometimes for many months, at the local inn, the Red Lion, whilst they underwent their treatment.

Writing in 1819, William Howitt describes a visit to Whitworth. "All about the village were wretched invalids walking, some with patched faces, some with an arm or a leg bound fast to a board – I suppose in order to straiten them; some with splints on their arm, shewing that they had been broken; others moving along slowly like spectres, in the lowest state of physical exhaustion, and others groaning inwardly as they passed, evidently from the tortures they were undergoing from the keen."

The 'keen' to which he refers was a caustic substance, which came in two varieties – red and white, that the doctors used to remove cancers. Their other remedies, all boiled up and prepared from local ingredients in the kitchen by Mrs George Taylor, included a herbal drink to purify the blood, a liniment called Red Rubbing Bottle, a black salve and copious quantities of snuff made from a rare woodland plant *Asarabacca Europaeum*, which grew locally. Asarabacca is the only British species of the Birthwort family. It is a curious plant consisting of a very short fleshy stem, bearing two large, dark-green, kidney-shaped evergreen leaves, and a solitary purplish-green drooping flower.

It was with snuff, made from the powdered dried leaves of this plant, that Dr John Taylor is reputed to have cured the Princess Elizabeth, daughter of George III and Queen Charlotte. The king had sent for John Taylor after he had cured a dying duchess, who was a lady in waiting to the queen, by lancing an abscess. The princess was suffering from constant pain in her head, probably a sinus condition, and the doctor administered snuff, which set off such a sneezing fit that her family became quite alarmed. "Let her sneeze," said the doctor, "that is the very thing that will do her good." And the remedy completely relieved the princess of her complaint.

The doctors specialised in the cure of cancers as well as setting broken bones and straightening limbs. William Howitt goes on to record the stories of two women patients. One bore the pain of the 'keen' for two to three hours daily and her cancer was successfully removed. Another woman, with breast cancer, travelled over a hundred miles to see Dr John Taylor, who, after examining her told her to return home as there was no hope that she could be cured. But she insisted that he tried, saying that she could bear any pain and was willing for the treatment to be 'kill or cure'. "Though art a brave lass," said John. "I will try." The lady stayed in Whitworth for six months and endured excruciating pain, but finally she was cured and lived for another thirty years.

The doctors treated all who came on a first-come first-seen basis, making no exceptions for the rich and titled who had to sit and wait with the rest. They charged everyone the same fee of eighteen pence a week, though the rich often gave donations and if someone was too poor to afford the fee they were never asked for the money. In fact there was subscription box for the support of those who were too poor to support themselves and John Taylor, as well as contributing himself, often took the box around to his wealthier patients and solicited contributions from them.

He was a down-to-earth man who didn't stand on ceremony, but treated everyone, rich and poor, high and low, in the same manner. One day, a nobleman brought his wife to see the doctor as she had been 'startled by a sudden fright, had fallen and from that time had been unable to put a foot on the ground'. John Taylor insisted that she

Whitworth House No.1 was the home of John Taylor, the first of the famous
Whitworth Doctors

try to walk, and as she struggled to stand, leaning on her husband, he ran up behind her and pushed her hard with his knee. The nobleman was incensed at this insult to his wife, but the doctor told him he was a fool. "Let the woman try to walk again," he said. And when she was eventually persuaded to try she found that she could. The doctor explained that the woman had dislocated her hip and that he had returned the joint to its correct position.

Amidst this curing of their human patients, the doctors also continued to treat animals, and in particular horses. In fact, some believed that the horses took precedence and there is a cartoon of John Taylor deserting Dr Thomas Thurlow, Bishop of Durham, in the middle of his treatment to rush outside to attend to a horse.

But another story illustrates both the caring nature of this man and the faith that people had in his abilities. One day a man brought two pitiable horses to the doctor. The man made his living by carting coal and although the two horses were worn out he couldn't afford to buy another so he asked the doctor if he could take the two horses and make one good one out of them. John told him to come back in a fortnight and when he did he presented him with a young and healthy horse of his own, but the man was not entirely satisfied. After examining the horse he said, "It's a wall'd eyed 'un. I canna abide a wall'd eyed 'un." But the doctor told him that he should have mentioned it before and it was too late to alter it now, and the man went off believing that the horse was a healthy compound of the two sickly ones he had brought. Though whether Dr John Taylor did it for the sake of the man or the sake of the horses will never be known.

John Taylor died on 26 January 1802, aged sixty-two years and his brother George died two years later. They are both buried at Whitworth. James Taylor (1768-1826), the son of John continued the practice and he was succeeded by his son George and then James Eastwood Taylor, who lived until 1876 and was the last of the Whitworth doctors.

Samuel Crompton

1753-1827

Inventor of The Mule

Samuel Crompton came from Bolton and was another inventor who helped to revolutionise the cotton industry, though he was a quiet and reticent person, not driven by the business acumen of Richard Arkwright. Although his invention of the spinning mule resulted in the Lancashire production of fine cotton cloth, that rivalled imported muslin from India, he did not end up a wealthy man.

Samuel Crompton was born on the 3 December 1753 at Firwood Fold. Like most families who were farmers the Cromptons also produced a small quantity of cloth by spinning and weaving, first wool and later cotton, on spindles and looms in their own home.

But the family wasn't well off. The farm which had once belonged to them had been mortgaged by Samuel's grandfather and sold by his father who subsequently lived there as a tenant. Soon after Samuel's birth the family moved from the farm to live at Hall-i'-th'-Wood in Bolton as caretakers.

Samuel Crompton © *Blackburn with Darwen Library and Information Services*

Then when Samuel was five his father died and his mother was left to bring up him and his two younger sisters, as well as caring for his disabled uncle, Alexander Crompton. She continued with some farming, making butter and honey, as well as spinning and weaving, and she managed to send Samuel to school where he was educated at the school of Mr Lever in Church Street under the well-known master, William Barlow.

But as soon as Samuel

was old enough he was expected to spin and weave as well. By the time he was fourteen he was spinning using the Spinning Jenny, working eight spindles at once, but he found that the thread often broke as he worked and he was increasingly frustrated by having to stop to mend the yarn. He began to wonder if he could find a better method of spinning the cotton to make it stronger.

He was good at making things and, following his father's musical interests, he had already succeeded in making and teaching himself to play a violin. And later he joined the Bolton Orchestra where he earned eighteen pence a night, which he used to buy tools to construct a new spinning machine.

Because he was already working hard during the day and in the evenings too, he worked on his spinning machine at night – causing local neighbours to wonder if Hall-i'-th'-Wood was haunted, as they heard strange noises and saw lights burning at all hours.

In 1721 a law had been passed to ban the import of Indian calicoes, in an attempt to protect the Lancashire spinning industry. But Indian muslins were still imported, and Samuel Crompton's aim was to construct a machine that would spin a cotton yarn even finer than the Spinning Jenny or the Water Frame. Such a yarn would be highly sought after as it would rival not only handspun yarns, but the expensive imported muslin as well, and it would enable Lancashire weavers to produce high volumes of cloth that would rival the Indian imports.

He worked on his invention from the age of twenty-two for five years. He worked in secret, first from his family, and later from the Luddites, whom he feared would break into the Hall and destroy his work. In fact he was so afraid that in one of the rooms he made a trap door and a hiding place, where his invention could be taken apart and hoisted into the roof space above the room.

But when the machine was complete and he began to produce yarn from it the secret was out. The first yarn he sold on Bolton market caused a sensation and Crompton and his wife, Mary Pimlott, who was also adept at spinning, were kept very busy.

However they were plagued by people who wanted to know more about this spinning machine that was at first called the Hall-i'-th'-Wood wheel, but later gained the nickname of the 'Mule' as it was a cross breed between the Spinning Jenny and the Water Frame. It managed to imitate the actions of the hand spinner by pulling and stretching the cotton as well as twisting it into a thread.

People tried to peer in through the windows at the spinning

process and it is said that some even climbed ladders to look through upstairs windows and that Samuel Crompton had to work behind a screen. One of his visitors was Richard Arkwright, who could well have given him some business advice, but unfortunately Samuel was out when he called.

Samuel Crompton had achieved what he had set out to do by making this machine. He wasn't interested in big business, just making a living for his family and he could not afford to patent the machine.

But he was so fed up with being pestered and spied on that he turned to a Bolton manufacturer, a Mr Pilkington, for advice – and his advice was that Samuel should give his invention away! And he not only gave away the secret of its workings, but he actually gave away the machine he was working on. In return he received a worthless written promise that eighty firms and individual manufacturers would pay a fee, which totalled just over £67. From this he only ever received around £50 – about enough money to allow him to build another Mule for his own use.

He moved his family from the Hall-i'-th'-Wood to a farmhouse at Sharples about two miles away, in an attempt to gain some peace and privacy. He was visited here by Sir Robert Peel. This was the first Sir Robert who lived from 1750 to 1830 and who had a calico printing firm at Church, near Accrington. It was his son, also Sir Robert Peel, who founded the police force. Sir Robert Peel tried to help Samuel Crompton by offering him a highly paid job with his firm. But Samuel refused, partly because he valued his independence and partly because he believed that Peel had insulted him on an earlier visit by offering him money to compensate him for the time he'd spent showing him the Mule.

So Samuel Crompton, his wife and their children continued in the same way that the family always had – farming, spinning and weaving on a small scale. And whilst he grew poorer, the cotton industry grew richer on his invention.

Sir Robert Peel tried his best to help him again and took Samuel to London to meet the Prime Minister, Spencer Perceval. In fact Spencer Perceval was discussing a payment of £20,000 to Samuel Crompton when he was shot dead in 1812 by John Bellingham, a failed merchant from Liverpool who blamed the prime minister for his financial difficulties.

A month later, Parliament voted to grant Samuel Crompton £5,000. He invested it in a bleaching works in Darwen and lost it all.

Samuel Crompton's grave in Bolton parish churchyard

In the end, he was reduced to such poverty that the firms who were using his Mule eventually examined their consciences and decided to make him a yearly payment of £63. He was only paid twice before he died in 1827. Thirty-five years later the people of Bolton decided to erect a statue in his memory. It cost £2,000.

Samuel Crompton is buried in the churchyard of St Peter's Church in Bolton. In 1861 local textile workers paid for a granite monument to be placed over his grave. The inscription reads: "Beneath this stone are interred the mortal remains of Samuel Crompton, of Bolton, late of Hall i'th' Wood, in the township of Tonge, inventor of the Spinning Machine called the Mule; who departed this life on the 26th day of June 1827, aged 72 years. Mors Ultimo Linea Rerum Est." The Latin means: "Death is the last boundary of human affairs".

The Hall-i'-th'-Wood was later abandoned and became derelict. It was bought by Lord Leverhulme who paid for it to be restored in memory of Samuel Crompton. In 1902 he gave the Hall to the people of Bolton and it's now open as a museum. It's situated on Crompton Way and inside you can see a working replica of the Mule.

Anne Cutler

1759-1794

Praying Nanny brought the hooligans to their knees

When people think of the Methodist Church and its inspirational preachers their minds mostly turn to John Wesley who founded the movement. But there were many other preachers who went around the country hoping for converts and when William Bramwell preached at Longridge, a young woman in the congregation, Anne Cutler, was deeply moved by his words.

She joined the Methodist movement, and although women preachers were not encouraged they were not barred and she felt called to overcome her natural shyness and become a preacher herself.

Anne was born at Thornley in 1759, where she worked as a handloom weaver and until the age of twenty-six had shown no particular interest in religion. But now she vowed herself to a life of celibacy, lived on a frugal diet of milk and herb tea, got up from her bed every night at midnight to pray and rose again at 4.00 a.m.

For nine years she lived a punishing lifestyle of physical exertion combined with little food and sleep, so perhaps it isn't surprising that she claimed to have seen visions. Despite the opposition of the Methodist leaders and attempts by her friends to dissuade her, 'Praying Nanny', as she became known, held a series of revivalist meetings throughout Yorkshire and Lancashire. She was responsible for many conversions, including some of the hooligans who turned up to disrupt her meetings.

In a letter to a friend from Manchester she wrote: "The last week but this at Oldham and Delph, and another place, and near a hundred souls were brought to God. Many cried for mercy and the Lord delivered them. In this town I cannot exactly tell the number. God has sanctified many; some preachers and leaders."

When she reached Macclesfield she became ill, but she continued to preach and pray, as well as visiting the sick. Many people, both rich and poor, sent for her as she travelled around. "The charm of her praying," says one of her biographers, "seemed to be in the intense force of her sympathy for the sinful, and for those who were immersed in the cares and pleasures of daily life."

But her self-imposed lifestyle meant that she was too weak to continue and she died a few days later at the young age of thirty-five. She was buried at Christ Church in Macclesfield and the inscription on her gravestone reads:

Underneath lie the remains of

ANNE CUTLER,
Whose simple manner, solid piety, and
Extraordinary power in prayer,
Distinguished and rendered her eminently
Useful in promoting a religious revival
Wherever she came.
She was born near Preston in Lancashire,
And died here December 29th, 1794.
Age 35.

Kitty Wilkinson

1785-1860

Fought for public baths and wash-houses

Although Catherine Seaward was born in Derry, in Ireland in 1785, she set sail for Liverpool with her parents, in search of a better life, when she was nine years old in 1794. The family, with Kitty, a younger brother and a baby sister set sail on a bright February morning, but their optimism about the future was to be short lived. As they approached the English coast a violent storm blew up and the ship became stranded on Hole Bank in the estuary of the River Dee. A boat was sent out to help the stricken passengers, and as a gale force wind blew and the waves raged Kitty and her mother and younger brother were rescued, but the baby was swept from Mrs Seaward's arms and washed away and no trace of her father was ever found.

And so Kitty's mother, whose health never recovered from the tragedy, found herself traumatised and alone in a strange city with two young children. The family was taken in by a Mrs Lightbody who lived in Denison Street and, as her mother could read and write and was a skilled spinner and lace maker, she was employed to teach her skills to the other servants. Although Mrs Lightbody was an elderly lady and was blind, she was keen to help others. Kitty later said that she was like a mother to her and her charitable example was to influence Kitty greatly as the years passed.

But the trauma that her mother had suffered caused her to have a breakdown and as she was unable to work or care for her children Kitty was sent to Caton, near Lancaster. Here she lived in the Apprentice House and worked in the cotton mill, where she stayed for ten years, the length of her indenture.

When she was twenty and free to leave she returned to Liverpool to care for her mother. They found accommodation in a house in Frederick Street and at first they both worked in domestic service. But Mrs Seaward's mental health was very fragile and at the age of twenty-five Kitty set up a small school in the house so that she could look after her mother as well as earn some money. The children were taught to read and write and sew. Mrs Seaward made lace during the day and Kitty sold this in the evenings after the day's lessons were over. For a while things appeared to be working out, but Mrs Seaward's health problems worsened. Her behaviour became violent and unpredictable and Kitty was forced to close her school.

For a while things weren't all bleak. In 1812, Kitty married a French sailor called Emanuel Demontee. The couple had a son, but just before the birth of their second child tragedy struck again when Emanuel was drowned at sea leaving her a widow. Kitty now had to work to support herself, her two sons and her sick mother, as the only other option was the workhouse.

She returned to domestic service, working for a family named Braik, who lived in Pit Street and Kitty soon found herself helping Mrs Braik with her charity work. When Mrs Braik died, she left instructions that her husband should provide for Kitty. Mr Braik bought Kitty a mangle so that she could work as a laundress. With the money she earned, she was able to rent a house in Denison Street, where she continued to help those less fortunate than herself by taking in orphans and sending as many as she could to be educated at the Bluecoat School.

In 1823 she married Tom Wilkinson, whom she'd first met at Caton. By this time Liverpool was becoming a wealthy city, but as the richer people moved to the outskirts the inner city living conditions deteriorated and in 1832 a cholera epidemic, partly caused by a lack of clean water and no facilities for washing, swept the city.

Tom and Kitty Wilkinson allowed all the families on their street to use their hot water boiler to wash bedding and clothes in an attempt to combat this deadly disease. They were also helped by support from the Liverpool District Provident Society and the Rathbone family, who each helped to provide clean clothes and fresh bedding to the poor. The washroom was moved from the cellar into the upstairs kitchen and the backyard was used to dry the washing. Families who could afford to were asked to contribute a penny towards the costs. Kitty also began another school, with the help of her neighbour, Mrs Lloyd, with lessons taking place in her own bedroom.

Because she understood that personal cleanliness and the washing of clothes and bedding were the best way to combat disease, Kitty Wilkinson fought for the provision of public baths and wash-houses to be established to combat dirt and disease and give the poor a better standard of hygiene and health. But it was not until 1842 that the first publicly funded washhouse was built in Upper Frederick Street in Liverpool. It was the first public baths and wash-house in the country.

In 1846 Kitty and Tom Wilkinson became Superintendents of the Frederick Street public baths and wash-house and, in the same year,

Kitty Wilkinson

at the age of sixty, Kitty was presented to Queen Victoria when she visited Liverpool.

By the turn of the century there were twelve baths and wash-houses in the city – including swimming pools as well as provision for bathing and washing – and Liverpool's first open air pool opened on Burlington Street in 1895.

Kitty Wilkinson did not live to see it. She died in 1860 at the age of seventy-three, but her memory lives on in a stained-glass window in Liverpool's Anglican Cathedral, which commemorates noble women.

Robert Peel

1788-1850

Founder of the modern police force

Probably the most famous of the Peel family, Robert Peel was the son of the first Sir Robert Peel (1750-1830) who was a partner in Haworth, Peel & Yates, the calico printing firm.

Robert (senior) married Ellen Yates the daughter of one of his partners and Robert (junior) was born at Chamber Hall near Bury on the 5 February, 1788. He was the third of eleven children and the eldest son and was described as being tall and thin in his youth with sandy coloured hair.

The family had made a fortune from their textile company and Robert was educated at home until he was ten years old by the Rev James Hargreaves. After his father's election as Member of Parliament for Tamworth in Staffordshire, the family moved to Drayton Manor in 1798 and he attended a small school there. From 1800 to 1804 he went to Harrow, followed by Christ Church College at Oxford, where he gained a Double First in Classics, and Mathematics and Physics. He was a distinguished student and was awarded an MA in 1814.

Like many politicians he began his career as a lawyer, but became MP for Cashel in County Tipperary in 1809, a seat bought for him by his father. There were only twenty-four voters and there was no contest for the seat. He rose quickly through the ranks of Tory government, first being appointed Under-Secretary for War and the Colonies. After Spencer Perceval, the Prime Minister, was shot dead in the lobby of the Houses of Parliament in May 1812, Robert Peel was given the job of Chief Secretary for Ireland – an unenviable task even in those days. It was here that his opposition to the Roman Catholic emancipation earned him the nickname 'Orange Peel'. He also became a Privy Counsellor. He moved to Dublin in September 1812 and stayed until 1818.

On his return to London in 1819 he chaired the enquiry into the return of the gold standard. In 1822 he became Home Secretary and immediately set about the task of updating criminal law. He repealed over two hundred and fifty statutes that had become outdated, including reducing the number of offences that carried the death penalty, and introduced eight new pieces of legislation. George Canning, who was Prime Minister from April 1827 until his death in

The statue of Robert Peel in Bury town centre

August the same year, said Robert Peel was 'the most efficient Home Secretary that this country ever saw'. But it is for his introduction of the foundations of the modern police force that he is best remembered. Constables had been appointed by courts around the country since medieval times. These men were responsible for bringing criminals to justice, but the job was unpaid and appointments were made yearly. Since around 1750 the Bow Street Magistrates Court in London had had uniformed 'Bow Street Runners' to catch criminals, and it was this idea that was expanded by Robert Peel. He had already established the Royal Irish Constabulary in 1812 and suggested setting up a force of paid constables in London, under the control of the Home Secretary, in an attempt to combat crime.

In 1829 the Metropolitan Police Act was passed and in September that year the first 'Peelers' or 'Bobbies' as they were called appeared on the streets, dressed in blue tailcoats and top hats to distinguish them from the red-coated soldiers with helmets. The Peelers were required to be as near to six feet tall as possible and were issued with a wooden truncheon, a pair of handcuffs and a wooden rattle to raise an alarm – though this was replaced by a whistle in the 1880s. They worked seven days a week with five days unpaid holiday each year and wore their uniforms both on and off duty. They were not allowed to vote in elections, and required permission to get married or even to share a meal with a civilian. They received one pound a week. At first they weren't popular and they weren't always successful, but they were the beginning of the modern police and other forces were begun across the country during Victorian times.

In 1830, Robert Peel (senior) died and Robert inherited the baronetcy and became the second Sir Robert Peel as well as taking over as Member of Parliament for Tamworth.

He became Prime Minister and Chancellor of the Exchequer on 10 December 1834 in a minority Tory government, but was forced to resign in April 1835. He became Prime Minister again in 1841, this time heading a majority government. He aimed to increase trade by removing import and export duties, believing that the increased prosperity would also help the poorest people. And for the first time in peacetime he introduced income tax.

But it was liberalism and concern for the common good that proved his undoing. Many of his own party opposed his liberal attitudes and he threatened to resign in 1844 if his Factory Act was not passed. His father had been partly responsible for the Factory Act of 1819, which forbade the employment in cotton mills of any child under nine, and limited the hours of those between nine and sixteen to twelve hours per day. The 1844 Factory Act reduced the working hours of children to six and a half each day, or ten hours every other day. It also forbade their use to clean under moving machinery – as the previous practice of sending small children to sweep cotton from underneath moving looms had resulted in many deaths and injuries.

His repeal of the Corn Laws in 1846 was the result of a long campaign by Manchester reformers to open up free trade and alleviate starvation in the county, as the removal of import tax on grain would result in cheaper bread. It was passed only because of the votes of the opposing Whig/Liberal party and the outcome enraged many Tories. Robert Peel resigned that same year and did not hold office again.

On 29 June 1850 he had a riding accident on Constitution Hill. Having fallen from his horse, the animal stumbled and fell on top of him and he died from his injuries a couple of days later on 2 July. He was buried in St Peter's churchyard at Drayton Bassett.

There is a bronze statue of Sir Robert Peel in Parliament Square, London. A similar statue was placed in the Market Place, near the Parish Church, in Bury in 1852. And there is another in Winckley Square in Preston.

A second local monument that honours Sir Robert Peel is the Peel Tower at Holcombe, which stands high on the hill and can be seen for many miles around. Built at a cost of £1,000, raised by public subscription, it is 128ft high and originally contained 148 steps. It was dedicated the day after the unveiling of the statue in Bury and there is a local tradition of walking up to the Peel Tower on Good Friday.

John Mercer

1791-1866

A love affair with colour

When you walk into a shop and see the racks of brightly coloured cotton T-shirts for sale you may be interested to know that you have Lancashire's John Mercer to thank for your wide choice.

He discovered the process of 'mercerisation', which was named after him, in 1844 – a process which allows cotton to be dyed successfully and which is still used in the production of the cloth today.

He was a self-taught chemist who was born on the 21 February, 1791 in Great Harwood. He began work at the age of nine as a bobbin winder and later went on to learn weaving. He had an older brother Thomas and a younger brother Richard. But when his father, Robert Mercer, died in 1802 John lived with various relatives until his mother married Thomas Mercer, who was no relation to his father, in 1806. In the same year, a half brother, William, was born.

John did not attend a school, but a neighbour, Mr Blenkinsop, taught him to read and write and some maths. He was later taught more mathematics by another friend, John Lightfoot.

John Mercer also taught himself to read music by matching hymn tunes that he knew well to the written marks on the paper. He would keep the piece of music he was working on pinned to his handloom so that he could study it as he worked.

He loved colour too and he became interested in the process of dyeing cloth, so he went into Blackburn to buy a chemistry textbook and some chemicals to make dyes. He taught himself the basics and set up a small business dyeing the cloth produced by other handloom weavers in the area. He loved experimenting and discovered a colour called antimony orange.

In 1814 John married Mary Wolstenholme and they had six children, although their first-born, Mary, only lived for a few days. Their second child was also a girl who was named Mary Clayton Mercer. She was also interested in science, but died at the age of nineteen. His four sons were all chemists too and there was another daughter, Maria, who died in 1913, aged ninety-three who left the money for the memorials that were built to her father. Strangely none of the children married.

Although he made other discoveries, including red ink and an

John Mercer *(reproduced by permission of Lancashire County Library – South East Division)*

'iron' medicine, it is for the process of mercerisation that John Mercer is mainly remembered. This is a process, still used today, that uses caustic soda to remove the water-resistant cuticle that covers cotton thread. Not only does this give the fibres a sheen, but it allows the dye to 'take' better and colour the cloth evenly. He discovered the process in 1844, and, after unsuccessfully trying to sell the secret of the process to the French, he patented it here and in the USA in 1851.

With his love of colour, John Mercer also became interested in colour photography. Although he did not manage to produce full-colour images, he did produce photographs on coloured cloth and coloured paper, and exhibited these at a meeting of the British Association in Leeds in 1858.

Although saddened by the death of his wife in 1859, he continued with his scientific research and was also appointed a Justice of the Peace in 1861 – though it is recorded that he preferred to forgive those brought before him rather than handing out punishments.

He also continued his scientific work and whilst collecting water samples from a nearby stream he slipped and fell in. He caught cold, never properly recovered and died the following year on the 30

November, 1866. He is buried at St Bartholomew's Church in Great Harwood.

Oaken Shaw Cottage, now known as Mercer House, where he lived, and its grounds, near Clayton-le-Moors were given as a museum and park to the people of Great Harwood. Mercer House can currently be hired as a venue for small meetings. Mercer Hall was built with the money left by Maria Mercer in 1913 and after the First World War it was eventually finished and opened in 1921. It was later converted into the swimming baths. The Memorial Clock Tower, unveiled in 1903, also remains as a reminder of John Mercer's love affair with colour that still brightens our lives today.

Joseph Livesey

1794-1884

Founder of the Temperance Movement

Joseph Livesey was born at 146 Victoria Road in Walton le Dale on 5 March 1794. Both his parents had died from a 'wasting sickness', possibly tuberculosis, by the time he was seven and he was brought up by his grandparents in a fairly poor household.

Joseph began his working life whilst still a child, winding bobbins for his grandfather and eventually became a hand loom weaver himself, working in the cellar of his grandparents' house and earning six shillings a week.

He married his wife, Jane, in Liverpool in May 1815. He had only met her three times before the wedding, but she had a reputation as an amiable and religious girl and he had decided that he would marry her before they even met the first time. They were married for fifty-three years and had thirteen children, though four died in infancy.

Joseph Livesey became a shrewd businessman and soon turned from handloom weaving to the more profitable business of selling cheese after he bought two whole cheeses from a farmer on Preston Market and sold them in portions, at a profit, from another stall. But his growing prosperity did not diminish his concern for those who were less well off. As he travelled around the local markets in Preston, Chorley, Blackburn and Wigan buying and selling cheese, he was distressed by the suffering he saw. The times were extremely hard before Robert Peel's repeal of the Corn Laws and bread had become so expensive that people were dying of starvation and those who lived were desperate and many sought solace in drink, especially gin.

One day in 1832, he was in the Cockpit Inn, behind the parish church in Preston, when a reformed alcoholic named Dicky Turner stood up to plead with people not just to give up gin and other spirits, but to give up all alcohol. It was said that because Dicky had a stammer, when he called for "t ... total abstinence" the slogan 'teetotal' was adopted on the spot.

Because of the poverty and suffering that Joseph Livesey saw around him he became an ardent lifelong campaigner for the temperance movement, trying to persuade people that drinking alcohol was not a solution to their problems and hardships.

He also gave practical assistance, forming a Relief Committee and in 1847, when unemployment was high, he created a scheme to employ men to repair the footpath that ran beside the River Ribble.

He also began a printing business producing leaflets, and the temperance journal *The Struggle* was the country's first illustrated halfpenny weekly. In it he criticised politicians and landowners for their role in taxing the poor and doing nothing to repeal the Corn Laws, which resulted in the extortionately high price of bread.

Joseph Livesey *(courtesy of the University of Central Lancashire Library Special Collections)*

The Struggle was published until 1844 when he established the *Preston Guardian*, forerunner of the *Lancashire Evening Post*. It related how crowds queued at soup kitchens for food, how children risked death by scavenging for coal on the railway, and how piles of goods, repossessed from the pawnshop were sold on the market for a few pence.

Joseph Livesey records how three bedsteads were sold for 11½d when most people slept on straw and how the old begged to be let into the dreaded workhouse rather than die on the street.

Livesey pointed out that those criminals who were in prison fared better than honest people, though many were in jail simply because they had no money to pay

The blue plaque that marks the site of the Cockpit Inn

their debts. And in Accrington people were so hungry that they dug up a sick and diseased cow that had died and been buried and ate it.

Joseph Livesey was part of a delegation that went to see Sir Robert Peel in 1842 to plead for his assistance in the repeal of the laws that prospered the rich whilst causing the poor to become poorer. Four years later the Corn Laws were repealed, but it cost Robert Peel the post of Prime Minister.

For twenty years, the Liveseys lived in a farmhouse at Holme Slack. They also built Lake View Villas at Bowness, where Jane died at the age of seventy-three. Afterwards, Joseph moved to 13 Bank Parade in Preston where he died in September, 1884 at the age of ninety. His funeral was attended by 10,000 people, including the mayor and other dignitaries and politicians. Flags were flown at half-mast from public buildings and the blinds were drawn at every house from Bank Parade to Preston cemetery where he was buried next to Jane. His epitaph reads: "He died in his ninety-first year after an honoured life of philanthropy and usefulness as author and worker, as the pioneer of temperance, the advocate of moral and social reform and the helper and friend of the poor".

During his lifetime he had been a great advocate of education as well as temperance. He and Jane taught many adults to read and write at their Sunday School and he promoted the Institution for the Diffusion of Knowledge founded by the Temperance Movement. This later became the Mechanics' Institute in Preston, forerunner of the Harris Institute which became Harris College in 1956, Preston Polytechnic in 1973 and is now the University of Central Lancashire. The university has an extensive archive of temperance memorabilia, including pledge cards, known as *The Livesey Collection*, which also contains some of Joseph Livesey's writings, his family Bible and his hymn book, a table made from Joseph Livesey's original handloom and oil portraits of both Joseph and Jane.

James Kay Shuttleworth

1804-1877

Reformer of the education system

He was born as James Phillips Kay in Rochdale on 20 July 1804. At the age of twenty-one he went to Edinburgh to train as a doctor and after qualifying in 1827 he returned to work in Manchester and within months found himself on the banks of the River Irwell trying to save lives following the horrendous disaster that followed the launch of the ship *Emma*.

There had never been a public launch of a ship onto the Irwell. When the New Quay Company announced that the fully rigged *Emma* would be launched on 19 February, 1828 crowds of workers deserted their jobs in the mills to watch the ship, with two to three hundred passengers aboard, all dressed in their best clothes, sail out onto the water. A band was playing, a cannon boomed and two ladies broke a bottle of wine over the ship's bows. But the *Emma* hurtled straight across the river, hit the opposite bank and keeled over, dumping all her passengers into the water. Several people stripped off their clothes, some of which had disappeared on their return, and jumped into the water to pull out body after body. And the young Dr James Kay was one the rescuers who bravely tried to resuscitate them by attempting to inflate their lungs with bellows and, it is recorded, giving blood transfusions from both men and dogs.

Two years later, in 1829, he was appointed as physician to the Ardwick and Ancoats Dispensary, which he had helped to set up and where he saw how the long hours that were forced on workers, along with their poor living conditions, were detrimental to their health. This was at the time when there was much unrest amongst the working class as the Corn Laws, which imposed a tax on imported corn, had combined with a poor harvest in 1816 to cause the price of bread to rapidly increase. Workers were demanding higher pay to buy food and there were strikes and food riots across the country. Kay realised that shorter working hours combined with education was one way to prevent the troubles escalating into full-scale rioting.

The Manchester Board of Health was set up with Kay as its secretary to clean up the slums and improve the living conditions of factory workers. Many people, at that time, had no access to clean drinking water and when cholera broke out in Manchester in 1832

Gawthorpe Hall

there were many deaths. Although Kay visited each of the city's four-teen district boards to assess the problem and record the spread of the disease, he was unable to establish its cause and it was twenty years later before polluted water was proven to be the reason.

Kay became a social reformer and he supported the repeal of the Corn Laws. In his pamphlet, 'The Moral and Physical Condition of the Working Classes Employed in the Cotton Manufacture in Manchester', he writes: "Prolonged and exhausting labour, contin-ued from day to day, and from year to year, is not calculated to develop the intellectual or moral faculties of man". He described how people worked in the mills from seven in the morning until seven at night, living on a diet of potatoes and bread before returning home to unsanitary, overcrowded houses, with no toilets. And recording the findings of the Board of Health he reports that: "Frequently, the Inspectors found two or more families crowded into one small house, containing only two apartments, one in which they slept, and another in which they ate; and often more than one family lived in a damp cellar, containing only one room, in whose pestilential atmosphere from twelve to sixteen persons were crowded. To these fertile sources of disease were sometimes added the keeping of pigs and other animals in the house, with other nuisances of the most revolting character."

After the passing of the 1834 Poor Law Amendment Act he became an Assistant Poor Law Commissioner, working in Norfolk, Suffolk and later in Middlesex and Surrey. He was also a great advocate of education and became the secretary to the committee of the Privy Council on Education in 1839. He helped to establish school inspectors and began the pupil-teacher system, where older pupils helped to teach the younger ones. In 1840, with the help of E.C. Tufnell, he also founded his own teacher training college, The Battersea Normal School (Teacher Training), which became St John's College, Battersea.

In 1842 he married Janet Shuttleworth who was the heiress to the Shuttleworth family of Gawthorpe Hall at Padiham near Burnley. He agreed to change his name to Kay Shuttleworth so that the family name would not be lost after their marriage, and it is by this name that he became known through his lectures and writing.

He wrote several other books and pamphlets on social reform including *Public Education* (1853), *Four Periods of Public Education* (1862) and *Thoughts and Suggestions on Social Problems* (1873). He also published two novels, *Scarsdale* (1860) and *Ribblesdale* (1874). He was a great friend and admirer of Charlotte Brontë who visited Gawthorpe Hall several times.

He retired in 1849, when he was knighted, and died in 1877.

William Harrison Ainsworth

1805-1882

Almost as popular as Charles Dickens

William Harrison Ainsworth is probably best known locally for his book *The Lancashire Witches* published in 1848, though this is by no means the only novel he wrote. His output totalled forty novels, including *Mervyn Clitheroe*, which was semi-autobiographical, and in his day he was almost as popular a writer as Charles Dickens.

Harrison Ainsworth was born on 4 February 1805 at 21 King Street in Manchester. His father's family could trace their ancestry back five hundred years to the Ainsworths of Tottington, and his mother's family could trace theirs back to Orme Touchet, who was a harpist to William the Conqueror.

From being a small child, Harrison Ainsworth loved stories and his father was an excellent storyteller and would often relate one which was a particular favourite about a robbery by Dick Turpin at Hough, near Rostherne in Cheshire, where his uncle lived and where Ainsworth stayed each summer. "Turpin was the hero of my boyhood," says Ainsworth. "When a boy I have often lingered by the side of the deep old road where the robbery was committed, to cast wistful glances into its mysterious windings, and when night deepened the shadows of the trees, have urged my horse on its journey, from a vague apprehension of a visit from the ghostly highwayman."

He attended the Manchester Free Grammar School and spent every moment of his spare time writing, poetry, stories and articles which were accepted by the *Edinburgh Magazine* and *Arliss's Magazine*.

When he left school at the age of seventeen, he was articled to a solicitor called Kay so that he could train as a lawyer and eventually join the family firm. But Kay became unhappy when he found that Ainsworth spent much of his time writing in the Chetham Library rather than studying the dusty legal texts that should have had his attention. And though there were many rows and recriminations, Ainsworth appears to have taken the criticism quite well.

"Mr Alexander Kay was anything but an idle man, and he became disgusted with his idle clerk," he said. And it seems his father agreed and is recorded as saying:

"He's an idle dog – he will never work."

But in June 1824 his father suddenly died and Harrison Ainsworth found that he was expected to take over as the head of the firm Ainsworth, Crossley and Sudlow. Knowing that he was woefully inadequate to do this, he went to London to complete his legal studies at the chambers of Mr John Phillips, a barrister and noted conveyancer.

At first he studied diligently, but the pleasures of London's literary society were an irresistible draw. He met John Ebers, who was a publisher and librarian. Ebers invited him to his house and here he fell in love with Ebers' younger daughter Fanny. She was said to be one of the most beautiful girls in London, though Harrison Ainsworth also had a reputation for his good looks so they must have made a beautiful couple. However, he kept the marriage a secret from his friends and family until two days before the wedding and only the bride's relatives were present at the ceremony.

Once married, he rejected the law to take over his father-in-law's publishing business – a step which not only meant resigning as a senior partner in his late father's firm but also losing the income that accompanied it. It must have also further alienated him from his family.

At first the business was successful, but Harrison Ainsworth was not a businessman and he began to concentrate on publishing books that he liked rather than those that would sell. In 1830, the year his third daughter was born, he gave up publishing and returned to practising law.

But Ainsworth retained his childhood capacity for imagination, as well as his interest in highwaymen. His first novel, *Rookwood*, published in 1843 and illustrated by George Cruikshank, tells the story of Dick Turpin's ride from London to York on his horse Black Bess. These hundred pages were written at one sitting in under twenty-four hours. "From the moment I got Turpin on the high road till I landed him at York, I wrote on and on without the slightest sense of effort," he records. Although he does add that he later made the journey himself to check on the distances and localities and was unsurprised at how accurate he was.

With this book Harrison Ainsworth achieved immediate fame. The fame promoted him into high society, where he became a fashion conscious celebrity, but his young wife was uncomfortable with this lifestyle and the marriage broke down after eight years. Fanny returned to her father's house where she died in 1838. Harrison Ainsworth went to live with relatives at Kensal Lodge and it was here that he held dinner parties that made it the most noted and popular literary venue in early Victorian times.

One evening he was introduced to a young man who was a reporter on *The Morning Chronicle* and was also contributing stories to *The Old Monthly Magazine* and *The Evening Chronicle*. Ainsworth was so impressed by his stories that he urged the young Charles Dickens to publish them in book form. It was also Ainsworth who introduced Dickens to the Grant brothers of Ramsbottom on whom he based the Cheeryble brothers in *Nicholas Nickleby*.

In 1848 Harrison Ainsworth published *The Lancashire Witches*, based on the account of the trials at Lancaster recorded by Thomas Potts, the Clerk to the Court. The book was accepted by *The Sunday Times* for serialisation and he was paid £1,000, which was a huge sum of money at that time.

Following this success he wrote many more novels, proving his father wrong in his assessment that he was an 'idle dog'. In the summer of 1853 he gave up his lavish London entertainments and went to live at Brighton to write. He remarried in 1878, although nothing is known about his second wife.

In 1881, Manchester gave a mayoral dinner in the Town Hall for him and honoured him with the title 'The Lancashire Novelist', though a guest at the event said that his "sad, resigned face, fringed by receding white hair and a white beard bears no recognisable relation-ship to the handsome young man whose picture was drawn by Maclise and D'Orsay in the 1820s and 1830s".

Three and a half months later, after living in semi-seclusion during much of his later life, he died at Reigate on 3 January 1882. He is buried in Kensal Green Cemetery, largely forgotten by modern readers.

Elizabeth Gaskell

1810-1865

Novelist inspired by social injustices

Born in Chelsea, London on 29 September 1810 as Elizabeth Stevenson, and brought up by her aunt, Hannah Lamb, at Knutsford in Cheshire, Elizabeth Gaskell is well remembered for her novels that drew from the social injustices she saw around her in industrial Manchester, where she lived for most of her life.

Elizabeth was the daughter of a Unitarian minister, William Stevenson and his wife, Elizabeth Holland. Her mother had given birth to a total of eight babies, but only Elizabeth and her brother, John, survived and when her mother died just over a year after her birth, Elizabeth was sent north to be raised by her mother's sister.

Unitarian families believed that it was important to educate girls as well as boys and Elizabeth had lessons at home up until the age of twelve when she was sent to the Byerley sisters' school at Barford, near Warwick. Here she learned Latin, French and Italian.

But it was after she had left school in 1827 that her brother John, who sailed for the East India Company, was lost at sea and she returned to London to nurse her grief-stricken father until his death in 1829.

After the death of her father she travelled to visit various relatives, but soon returned north where she met William Gaskell, who was also a Unitarian minister. The couple married in 1832, when Elizabeth was twenty-two, and they came to live in Manchester, where William was the minister at Cross Street Chapel. The city was to be her home for the rest of her life.

Here she taught at Sunday Schools and evening classes, provided for working class children and, as the wife of the minister, Elizabeth saw much that shocked her in the city, including the poverty and poor living conditions of many of the parishioners. Children were dying from disease and hunger.

Four of the Gaskells' daughters survived, but it was after the death of their only son, William, whilst he was still a baby in 1845 that, encouraged by her husband, she wrote her first novel *Mary Barton: A Tale of Manchester Life* which was published in 1848 and highlighted the plight of the textile workers. Many readers found the book shocking and it was criticised for having 'unsuitable' subject matter and was even considered by some to be subversive. And many Manchester mill owners attacked the book as irresponsible and misguided. It was banned from some public libraries and even burnt by protesters.

Following its publication she was invited by Charles Dickens to contribute to his magazine *Household Words*, where her next novel, *Cranford*, was first published in serial form between 1851 and 1853. She also wrote short stories, essays and articles for magazines. However, she didn't shut herself away in a study, but wrote on a corner of the dining room table whenever she could snatch a few moments from her busy life.

North and South, published in 1855, continued the theme of the clash between the industrialised north and the more genteel south. For this Elizabeth Gaskell drew on her own personal experiences of crossing cultural and social divisions.

Through her work and writing she also became a friend of Charlotte Brontë. And after Charlotte's premature death in 1855, her father, Patrick Brontë, asked Elizabeth to write her biography. Her *Life of Charlotte Brontë*, published in 1857, created some controversy and threats of libel action because of some of the things she had said about Branwell Brontë's love affair with Mrs Robinson and about the Cowan Bridge School, which was the inspiration for

Elizabeth Gaskell *(courtesy of Manchester Archives and Local Studies Library)*

Lowood in *Jane Eyre*. These were removed before the publication of a new edition and there was an apology for the original version in *The Times*, although Elizabeth was in Italy at the time and knew nothing of it.

Her later books though were not so controversial. She wrote *Sylvia's Lovers* in 1863, which was about the repercussions of the Napoleonic Wars, *Cousin Phyllis* in 1863, and *Wives and Daughters*, about the lives of country families – though she died before she had finished writing it. She had only a few pages left to finish when she died on 12 November 1865. Sitting around the fire with her daughters, after tea one afternoon, she died suddenly of a heart attack at the age of fifty-five. She was buried in the Unitarian Churchyard at Knutsford.

Henry Tate

1819-1899

A fortune from sugar lumps

Think of Henry Tate and you probably already know about Tate & Lyle the sugar refiners and you're sure to have heard of the Tate Gallery, but did you know that Henry Tate was a Lancastrian and that his fortune was made by producing sugar lumps?

He was born in Chorley on 11 March 1819 and was the son of the Rev William Tate, a Unitarian minister. When he was thirteen he became an apprentice in the grocery trade in Liverpool and, after serving his seven-year apprenticeship, he set up his own business in Old Haymarket in Liverpool in 1839. In 1847 he opened a second shop in Old Hall Street, followed by another shop in Liverpool and one in Church Street in Ormskirk.

Eventually he had a total of six shops in his empire, but he sold them all in 1859 to go into partnership with John Wright & Co, sugar refiners. After the death of John Wright in 1869 the partnership was dissolved and he began his own sugar refining business, which became Henry Tate and Sons.

Henry Tate was a talented entrepreneur with an eye for innovations. During the building of a new sugar refinery in Love Lane in 1872, he adapted the plans to

Henry Tate *(photograph courtesy of Lancashire County Library)*

use the new Boivin-Loiseau method of refining, which increased the yield of white sugar. When the refinery became operational in 1872, it was producing 400 tons of sugar a week.

In 1875 he bought the patent from a German inventor named Eugen Langen for a machine which he used to manufacture sugar cubes. Before this, sugar was produced and sold in large blocks or loaves and had to be cut into small pieces with domestic 'sugar nippers', and it was the production of ready cut 'sugar lumps' that made his fortune.

Around 1878 he established the Thames Refinery at Silvertown in East London which specialised in producing cubed sugar. In 1881 he moved from Liverpool, leaving his two sons, Alfred and Edwin, in charge of the business there, to live in London at Park Hill in Stratham. It was here that he established the first Tate Gallery.

In 1891 he was given the Freedom of the City of Liverpool and was knighted in 1898. He died on 5 December 1899 and his company was amalgamated with the Abram Lyle company in 1921 to form Tate & Lyle, on the understanding that Tate would produce sugar cubes and Lyle would specialise in Golden Syrup, even though the refineries were only one mile apart in London.

As well as being known for his sugar refining, Henry Tate is remembered as a generous philanthropist. He gave substantial amounts of money to the Hahnemann Hospital, and Liverpool Royal Infirmary as well as University College, Liverpool, the forerunner of Liverpool University. He gave £500 towards books for a new library in Chorley in 1899. He also donated towards the building of libraries at Streatham, Lambeth and Brixton, and the 'Tate Institute' at Silvertown, North Thames, which was 'for the benefit of the industrial classes'.

But it is with art galleries that his name is mostly associated. Henry Tate first displayed paintings and sculpture by leading contemporary artists at his London home. When he became short of space he offered his collection to the National Gallery, but they did not have the space to exhibit the whole collection either, so he offered to build a new gallery if the government would provide a place for it. The Chancellor of the Exchequer offered a site at Millbank, where the Millbank Prison had been demolished, and the gallery known as the National Gallery of British Art was built at a cost of £80,000. It opened on 21 July 1897, containing sixty-five pictures donated by Henry Tate, and soon became better known as the Tate Gallery. At that time it displayed only modern British art, defined then as artists born after 1790, but in 1917 the gallery was also made responsible for the national collection of international modern art and for British art going back to the 1500s.

In 1988, the Tate Gallery at the Albert Dock in Liverpool was opened to increase public awareness of and access to the collections that were formerly only on view in London. Today, what was the Tate Gallery has become Tate, a family of four galleries: Tate Britain and Tate Modern in London, Tate Liverpool and Tate St Ives.

Henry Tate is buried in West Norwood Cemetery, near where he lived at Park Hill.

Edward Graham Paley and Hubert James Austen

1823-1895 and 1841-1915

Architects of Lancashire churches

During Victorian times there was much church building, mostly with money donated by businessmen who had made their fortunes during the Industrial Revolution and who desired to leave a lasting memorial to their wealth.

In Lancashire, many of these new churches were designed by the Lancaster firm of architects, Sharpe, Paley and Austen, who undertook over six hundred commissions between 1836 and 1942, ranging from churches to railway stations and hospitals.

The firm was founded by Edmund Sharpe in 1836 and he was joined by Edward Paley in 1845. However, Sharpe retired soon after and when Hubert Austen teamed up with Paley in 1868 the two men worked together, building not only churches but a reputation for quality.

Edward Graham Paley was born in 1823. He was the fourth son of a clergyman and grandson of Archdeacon Paley, and was born at Easingwold vicarage. In 1838, he joined Edmund Sharpe as a pupil before rising to become his partner and then running the firm alone until he was joined by Hubert Austen. He served as a council member of the Royal Institute of British Architects, and as an examiner and a member of the Royal Archaeological Society. He was also involved in many local institutions and associations including the planning committee for the Royal Albert Institution and the Infirmary, Art Education, the Mechanics Institute and later the Storey Institute, the Rowing Club, and the Choral Society. He was a regular worshipper at Lancaster Priory and later at Caton Parish Church.

In 1851 he married Fanny Sharpe who was the sister of Edmund Sharpe and they had a son, Harry, who later joined the practice. The couple also had three daughters.

As well as having a country house called Moorgarth at Caton, he designed and built a house called The Greaves between Lancaster and Scotforth where he died in 1895.

Hubert James Austen was born in 1841 and was also the son of a clergyman. His father was the Rector of Redmarshall, County

St Peter's RC Lancaster Cathedral was designed by Paley and Austen

Durham. He began his career in architecture with his half brother Tom, who was a pupil of Sharpe and Paley in the 1850s, but then joined George Gilbert Scott as his pupil.

His return to the firm in 1868 helped it to build on its success and gain a reputation for church design in the Gothic style. Austen specialised in church architecture and designed over a hundred new churches in the Decorated and Perpendicular styles as well as advising on many restorations, where his knowledge of medieval architecture was invaluable.

He was a church-warden at Lancaster Priory and he was involved in alterations there, including the King's Own Memorial Chapel and a new porch built in memory of his wife's parents in 1903.

He was a great music lover too, and was a member of the Lancaster Choral and Orchestral Societies. Other hobbies included sketching, painting and gardening. His wife was also named Fanny and was a niece of Edmund Sharpe, so the firm really was a family affair. The couple had two sons and four daughters and their house, designed by Austen, was The Knoll on Westbourne Road in Lancaster where he died in 1915. He also had a country house, Heversham Hall, in Cumbria and another near Winchester named Kingsworthy Court.

Paley and Austin's work had a huge effect on the prosperity of

Edward Graham Paley *(photograph courtesy of Lancashire County Library)*

Lancaster as income was generated for many local firms who worked as contractors, providing not only builders but many specialist tradesmen such as Gillows for ecclesiastical woodwork and Shrigley & Hunt for stained glass. Slates, bricks, stone and timber also needed to be supplied along with plumbers, electricians and many other skilled workers and manufacturers.

Paley and Austen entered the Carlisle Diocesan Competition for Mountain Churches, which led to the building of Torver and Finsthwaite churches. Later they entered the competition for the new Liverpool Anglican Cathedral, to be beaten by Giles Gilbert Scott, the grandson of George Gilbert Scott

Paley and Austen worked together until they were joined by Paley's son, Henry, in 1886. Austen's son, Geoffrey, also joined the firm in 1914, but was called up to serve in the First World War the following year; Henry (Harry) Paley ran the business until he died at the age of eighty-five in 1944.

During the years that the firm was in business the architects created 370 major works, 148 restorations and 118 minor works, mostly in Lancashire. Examples of their work include St Peter's RC Church in Lancaster, which became the Cathedral of the Diocese of Lancaster in 1924. Designed by Edward Paley in the Gothic style, it is built of local stone, has a 250ft-high spire which houses ten bells and was opened by Bishop Goss of Liverpool in 1859.

When Lancaster decided to improve the Town Hall, the Town Hall Improvement Committee appointed Paley and Austen to be their architects in October 1870. They added a large extension in New Street as well as accommodation for the Superintendent of Police and his family. And after a fire at Holker Hall, which destroyed the west wing, the owner, William Cavendish, the 7th Duke of Devonshire, called in Paley and Austen. The rebuilt wing in red sandstone was described by Pevsner as 'the best Elizabethan Gothic in the north of England'. It is now open to the public.

The names of Paley and Austen are not very well-known, but Nikolaus Pevsner, who was often critical of Victorian architects, describes them as being 'of the highest European Standard of their years'. As some of their designs are now in need of repair it would be a shame if they faced demolition instead of being preserved as examples of the work of Edward Paley and Hubert Austen.

William Pickles Hartley

1846-1922

Famous for his jams and preserves

William Pickles Hartley was born in 1846 in Colne and his name is still seen today on the jars of jam that line the supermarket shelves.

The Hartley family had lived in the Pendle area since around 1620 and were the builders of nearby Wycoller Hall – famous as the inspiration for Fearndean Manor in Charlotte Brontë's *Jane Eyre*. They moved into the grocery trade, beginning with small shops but later becoming wholesale grocers.

William Hartley left the Grammar School at the age of fifteen to work in the family business. One day, so the story goes, a supplier failed to deliver a batch of jam to the shop and William's solution was to make some of his own. His jam sold so well that he decided to continue making it, along with marmalade and jelly. He later expanded his business by moving into fruit preserving, which he packed into earthenware jars for sale.

William Hartley married Martha Horsfield and in 1880 the family moved to Southport. They had five daughters and a son John. One daughter, Christiana, became the Mayor of Southport in 1921 – the first woman to do so.

In the 1881 Census he is recorded as: 'William Pickles HARTLEY, Male, 35. Colne, Lancashire, England. Occupation: Wholesale Preserve Manufacturer, Employing On Average 120 Women & 30 Men'.

In 1884 the jam making business became William Hartley & Sons Ltd and the following year it was relocated to Aintree near Liverpool where he built Hartley Village for his workers. And in 1902 he opened a jam factory in Bermondsey, London, which employed over 2,000 workers.

By 1908 he had been knighted by King Edward VII for his many charitable acts. William Hartley gave money to Colne, Liverpool and London for the establishment of schools and hospitals. In 1914 he bought a four and a half acre site at Colne and paid for the building of a new hospital. The work though was delayed by the First World War and did not begin until 1920. Sir William, as he had become by then, laid the foundation stone at a ceremony that attracted 'a great gathering of townspeople' in 1921, though he died the following year and did not live to see Hartley Hospital opened. In the 1980s the former Burnley Health Authority decided to close the hospital and move its services to Burnley General despite a long campaign to save it. The site has since been redeveloped as residential housing and is called Hartley Gardens.

The name of Hartley is evident all around Colne and the name was also used for the fictional setting of the television series *Juliet Bravo* that was filmed in the region.

William Pickles Hartley died in 1922.

Frances Hodgson Burnett

1849-1924

Author of 'The Secret Garden' and 'Little Lord Fauntleroy'

Frances Hodgson Burnett, the author of the well-known children's stories *The Secret Garden* and *Little Lord Fauntleroy* is often presumed to be an American by birth. In fact she was born in Cheetham Hill, Manchester on 24 November 1849 as Frances Eliza Hodgson.

Following her father's death in 1854, Frances' mother struggled to keep herself and her five children as well as continuing to run the family business, a wholesale firm that supplied art materials to wealthy manufacturers. But after the promise of support from a maternal uncle wasn't forthcoming, the family emigrated to Knoxville in Texas, USA in 1865.

It was here that the young Frances began to write short stories. She sent her first submission to an editor after earning the money for the paper and postage by picking and selling wild grapes.

Her first successes came just three years later with *Hearts and Diamonds* and *Miss Cauther's Engagement* being published in Godey's *Lady's Book*. Soon her work was being regularly published in *Scribner's Monthly*, *Peterson's Ladies' Monthly* and *Harper's Bazaar*. She wrote five or six stories every month and sold them for $10 each, which she used to support her family.

She married Dr Swan M. Burnett of Washington D.C. in 1873. She had known him since she was fifteen years old and following a honeymoon that was combined with a business trip to New York, her first child, Lionel, was born in 1874 and her second son Vivian was born during a trip to Paris.

Her reputation as a novelist was made at this time, when her story of a pit girl in Lancashire, *That Lass o' Lowrie's* was published and serialised in *Scribner's Monthly* in 1877.

During her lifetime it was her romantic novels that made her popular. After the family settled in Washington in 1877 she wrote *Haworth's* in 1879, *Louisiana* in 1880, *A Fair Barbarian* in 1881, and *Through One Administration* in 1883, as well as a play, *Esmeralda*, written in 1881 with William Gillette.

Nowadays it is for her children's stories that she is best remembered. *Little Lord Fauntleroy*, the story of an American boy who discovers he is an English lord, was published in 1886. The character with his long blond curls was based on her younger son Vivian and his velvet suits with lace collars were inspired by the dress sense of Oscar Wilde. The book sold more than half a million copies, made her $100,000 and prompted many mothers to dress their sons like the main character in the book!

Other popular children's stories followed with *Sara Crew* in 1888, which was dramatised as *A Little Princess* in 1909 and is the story of an orphan who is forced to work for the headmistress of a seminary school after her father dies, and the ever-popular *The Secret Garden*, also published in 1909.

In 1888 she won a court case in the UK over the dramatic rights to *Little Lord Fauntleroy* and established a precedent that was incorporated into British copyright law in 1911. When she published *Haworth's* in 1879 she had travelled to Canada on the day of the British publication to protect her legal rights to British copyright and royalties by standing on British soil. But the copyright laws did not apply to plays and until this court case there had been nothing to stop British playwrights taking her stories and turning them into stage productions for which she received no payment. So when, in 1887, she came to London with her sons and a friend for the Golden Jubilee of Queen Victoria and discovered that a stage version of *Little Lord Fauntleroy*, dramatised by Seebohm, was to open soon without her permission, she decided to write her own version. Her version opened three months later in May 1888 starring the famous child actress Vera Beringer and received better reviews. Frances sued Seebohm, and the judge ruled in her favour. The Society of British Authors arranged a dinner to honour her and presented her with a diamond ring and bracelet as well as a certificate of thanks.

The successful court case made her an international celebrity and the lives of herself and her family were reported in newspapers. But as happens with celebrity it wasn't long before the press turned against her, criticising her books, her trips abroad, her clothes and her family, and linking her name romantically with a series of men. She suffered from poor health and depression. Her elder son Lionel died from tuberculosis in 1890 and she was divorced from her first husband in 1898. In 1900 she married Stephen Townsend, who was her business manager and who also collaborated with her to write several plays, though there was a rumour that he blackmailed her into this second marriage which ended in 1902.

During this time she lived mainly in England, though Frances became a US citizen in 1905 and returned to live in the USA in 1909. In later years, with public opinion set against her, she lived in seclusion and her last public appearance was at the screening of the film version of *Little Lord Fauntleroy* in 1921, starring Mary Pickford as Cedric.

Frances Hodgson Burnett died on 29 October, 1924 in New York and is buried in Roslyn Cemetery. Her son Vivian is buried beside her and a life-size effigy of Lionel stands at their feet.

William Hesketh Lever

1851-1925

Lancastrian philanthropist

You may not know the name William Hesketh Lever, but you will probably have heard of Sunlight Soap.

William Lever, the soap's manufacturer, was born at 6 Wood Street in Bolton on 19 September 1851. He was the son and heir that his parents had longed for after the birth of six daughters, though his parents went on to have three more children including another son. His father was a wholesale grocer, with his business on Bank Street in Bolton, and William's first job when he began work for the family firm was to cut and wrap chunks of soap from a large block.

After a couple of years' work experience, during which time he married his childhood friend, Elizabeth Ellen Hulme, at St George's Congregational Church, Bolton, William became a salesman. It was then that he realised there was a market for pre-packaged quality soap and so he went into partnership with his younger brother, James, and leased a factory in Warrington, where they founded Lever Brothers and registered the brand name 'Sunlight'.

In 1887, needing to expand the business, he looked around for a suitable new site for his factory. The site needed to be near the River Mersey for the importing of raw materials and near a railway line for the transportation of the finished products. The marshy, uninspiring ground that he discovered was eventually transformed into the village

William Hesketh Lever *(photograph courtesy of Lancashire County Library)*

of Port Sunlight, which was named after his famous soap. Here, he not only built a factory, but a garden village for the workers to provide them with good living conditions, including amenities such as the Lever Free Library, an open air heated swimming pool, shops, an auditorium, a technical institute and, of course, a church – Christ Church, built in 1904.

One of his many interests was architecture and he drew the original plans for Port Sunlight himself before employing nearly thirty different architects to create its unique style.

The welfare of his workforce was paramount. There was a cottage hospital in the village, which treated workers until the introduction of the National Health Service in 1948. He also encouraged sports, games, education and an interest in art, literature, science and music. Many clubs and societies flourished in the village, including The Boys' Brigade, the Port Sunlight Players and many sports clubs. Though, as William Lever was opposed to alcohol, The Bridge Inn opened in 1900 as a temperance hotel. He also ventured into politics and was elected Member of Parliament for the Wirral in 1906.

He was very interested in art and collecting, and he believed that art and education should be freely available to everyone. He opened a museum at Port Sunlight in 1903 and later, in 1922, the Lady Lever Art Gallery, in memory of his wife, who died in 1913 and whom he sorely missed.

"I am convinced that without her great influence there would have been neither a Port Sunlight, nor a Lever Brothers as we know it today," he said.

The village is now a conservation area, with nearly all the buildings being Grade II listed and of great architectural importance. The gallery is open to the public and houses a varied collection of paintings, furniture and porcelain.

William Lever also had a country retreat at Rivington where he created a huge garden on land close to the village. He bought the 2,100 acres that made up the Rivington Hall Estate from John.W. Crompton in 1899 for £60,000, with the agreement that the Crompton family could continue to live at Rivington Hall. He kept forty-five acres for his own use and donated the rest, to be known as Lever Park, to Bolton Corporation in 1902.

With his passion for architecture and landscape design, Lever set about building Roynton Cottage, a timber bungalow that he planned to use as a weekend retreat.

In 1905 work began to create formal gardens around the bungalow.

With the assistance of T.H. Mawson, a landscape architect, the transformation began of the wild moorland, work that was to continue for the rest of his lifetime. First the Great Lawn was laid out below the bungalow. Then, in 1910, the Pigeon Tower was built along with terraces and garden shelters. Ornamental doves and pigeons were housed here and his wife would climb to the top floor to enjoy the view whilst she did her sewing. Today, many of the shelters still remain and the Pigeon Tower was restored from a ruined shell in 1975, at a cost of £5,000, by the North West Water Authority.

Just below was a swimming pool where William Lever would take an early morning dip! Trees and shrubs, both native and exotic were planted and an army of gardeners was employed to tend them. And not even the destruction of the original Roynton Cottage deterred him. As an MP he was an ideal target for women demanding the right to vote and Mrs Edith Rigby, a very determined suffragette, set fire to his weekend home on the night of 7 July 1913 and it was totally destroyed. So a new, altogether grander, bungalow was built from local stone at a cost £30,000 and included a circular ballroom, forty-four feet in diameter with a sprung floor of polished oak parquetry and a domed glass ceiling. Sadly only some old photographs and a few areas of black and white floor tiles amid the grass and mud are all that remain now.

Work went on in the gardens year after year as they were continually extended and improved. In 1921 The Ravine was constructed, surrounded by terraces and crossed by a footbridge. If you didn't know better, you would never think that this was a man-made feature. The waterfalls and rockpools appear entirely natural as the water cascades down the hillside.

Then, in 1922, came the Japanese Garden. Following a visit to Japan by Lever, Mawson helped him to re-create a taste of the Orient on a bleak Lancashire hillside, complete with tea houses, lanterns and an ornamental lake, inhabited by flamingos, swans and ducks. Now, by the side of the path as you approach the lake, you can still see the stone base of a huge lantern as well as the stone bases where the teahouses once stood around the lake.

Work continued on the gardens until his death in 1925 at the age of seventy-four, when death duties forced the sale of the bungalow and gardens to J. Magee a local brewery owner. But, although overgrown, the gardens are now accessible to the public and provide a picturesque walk at any time of the year.

Although he became very wealthy William Lever adhered to a

simple, and somewhat austere, lifestyle. He eschewed drinking, smoking and gambling, and on a typical day it is said that he would rise at 5.00 a.m. in his open-air bedroom, that was little more than a glass roof with open sides, exercise, take a cold shower and work until 5.30 p.m., taking only a fifteen-minute lunch break.

But he was a philanthropist who loved to give money to schemes that would benefit society. As well as donating Lever Park to the people of Bolton, he was a governor of Bolton School and established the Lever Trust for the Girls' School in Bolton, as well as giving money to the Universities of Liverpool, Edinburgh and Bristol. He also bought Hall i' th' Wood, a fifteenth-century half-timbered manor house at Bolton which had fallen into disrepair, paid for its restoration in memory of Samuel Crompton, the inventor of the Spinning Mule who had lived there with his parents and in 1902 he gave the Hall to the people of Bolton.

He was created a baronet in 1911 and became Sir William Lever. He was Mayor of Bolton during 1918 to 1919, with his daughter-in-law filling the role of Mayoress. In 1922 he was made a Viscount, and became Viscount Leverhulme of the Western Isles. He also bought land in the Hebrides and ventured into commercial fishing, founding Mac Fisheries which had shops in all the major towns.

A portrait of Lord Leverhulme was painted by Augustus John in 1920, but he did not want anyone to see it and as it was too big to fit in his safe he cut out the face and locked that away. The two parts were rejoined in 1954 and the portrait now hangs in the Lady Lever Art Gallery where the signs of its restoration can be clearly seen.

Lord Leverhulme died on 7 May 1925 at The Hill, his London home, soon after his return from a world tour. He is buried next to his wife at Christ Church in Port Sunlight.

In his will he left a proportion of his interest in the company he founded in trust for 'the provision of "scholarships for the purposes of research and education."' So The Leverhulme Trust was established, which now gives grants and awards for a wide range of educational and research purposes totalling around £25 million a year.

Edith Rigby

1872-1948

An unconventional campaigner for women's rights

The Preston born suffragette, Edith Rigby, liked to be known as Mrs Edith Rigby. More conventionally she would have been known as Mrs Charles Rigby, the doctor's wife, as a woman should only revert to her own Christian name on becoming a widow. But Edith wasn't prepared to wait that long to regain her own identity.

Born Edith Rayner at 1 Pole Street, Preston in 1872, she was the second of seven children born to Dr Charles Rayner. Her brother Arthur also became a doctor and he founded the X-ray department at Preston Royal Infirmary.

She was a pretty child who apparently grew to be a strikingly beautiful woman, with golden hair and intense blue eyes, though she rarely allowed herself to be photographed. Her concerns lay with others rather than herself and many people regarded her as being rather odd and eccentric.

Her different way of looking at life, and in particular the role of women, was evident from an early age. Even as a child she questioned the division between the working women with their clogs and shawls and the ladies of leisure who paraded through Miller Park in their silks and satins.

On the Christmas morning after her twelfth birthday, Edith was missing from the house when her family got up. She arrived home later to explain to her parents that she had been out distributing small gifts of chocolate, soap and candied fruit that she had been collecting over the preceding weeks to work people in the streets as they made their way to church.

The desire to help others was one that stayed with Edith Rigby all her life, although it is her newsworthy exploits in the pursuance of votes for women for which she is most readily remembered.

Less is known about her life-long love of fell walking, her distaste of having skirts flapping around her ankles, her penchant for wearing only sandals on her feet and her prowess as a swimmer and the fact that she was the first lady in Preston to ride a bicycle, in bloomers, a habit which was regarded as being improper and for which she was booed and pelted with vegetables.

Although Edith showed far more interest in other's welfare than

The house on Winckley Square, Preston where Edith Rigby lived

she ever did in men, her extreme beauty brought many admirers and in September 1893, a month before her twenty-first birthday she married thirty-four year old Dr Charles Rigby and went to live with him at 28 Winckley Square, Preston. But her marriage was far from conventional. Edith did not take on the role of a middle class married woman, but busied herself trying to improve working conditions for girls and women in the local mills. She also continued her own style of living by buying a bungalow at nearby Broughton where she grew fruit and vegetables.

About this time she began a club for girls, at St Peter's School in Brook Street, where they could meet to sew, sing, play games and continue with an education that was curtailed for most of them at the age of eleven when they began to work part-time in the mills. Edith taught them about hygiene, took them swimming, taught them to play cricket in the park and bullied the owners of large country houses to hold garden parties on summer Saturday afternoons.

But it is for her involvement with the suffrage movement that Edith Rigby is best known. Never one to take up a cause without giving it her best attention, Edith is famous for the burning of Lord Leverhulme's bungalow at Rivington and her hunger strikes which accompanied her many episodes of imprisonment.

Edith was sent to prison the first time after rising at half past five one sleety morning in February 1907 to take part in a suffragette march from Hyde Park to Caxton Hall, where the protestors tried to form a 'Women's Parliament'. Edith, along with Christabel and Sylvia Pankhurst and a handful of other women, continued the protest to the Houses of Parliament, but rows of police forced them back to Caxton Hall, where fighting broke out and fifty-seven women were arrested. Given a choice between paying a fine or serving a month in prison, they all chose prison and Edith, who had been a prison visitor at Preston gaol, now found herself on the other side of the bars.

"Prison is hopeless as a place of reform," she told a press reporter on her release. And it certainly didn't change Edith Rigby, because she went there again and again.

The hunger strikes were begun by a Miss Dunlop who refused to eat when her request to be treated as a political prisoner was denied. She fasted for four days of her month long sentence and was released. The suffragettes realised that this was a powerful weapon and from then on hunger strike was the unspoken order. And the government, given the choice of enfranchising women or letting them die, began a regime of force-feeding.

Hunger strikers who resisted were held down by four wardresses while a doctor inserted a tube down their throats and a fifth wardress would pour in liquid. Later, when even this barbaric treatment failed to deter women from their aim, an Act of 'cat and mouse' was introduced, where women in danger of death after several days with neither food nor water, were released to recover their health before being re-arrested to continue their sentences. On one occasion when the police called at Winckley Square to re-arrest Edith under this Act, she escaped from the back door in workmen's clothes and rode off on her bicycle.

Despite all the campaigning and arson and imprisonments, it was probably the First World War that was the catalyst for some women at least to gain the vote. In 1914 an uneasy truce was called between the suffragettes and the government. The country needed women to fill the jobs of the men who had gone to fight. Nine months after the Armistice women over thirty who were local government electors (or wives of electors) were placed on the voters' register, but it wasn't until 1928 that women were allowed to vote on equal terms with men.

After the war, Edith Rigby turned to farming and became increasingly interested in the teachings of Rudolph Steiner. One of her

The blue plaque that marks Edith Rigby's residence

friends commented, "After the vote was won she gave up all her good works and took up with Rudolph Steiner."

She cut her hair short, wore men's clothes and spent most of her time working on her small-holding where she grew fruit and vegetables and kept animals and bees. Her methods nowadays would be called organic and following Steiner's teachings she strove to produce good wholesome food, using no artificial means.

Strangely, her marriage to Charles Rigby was a happy one. He eventually retired and went to live with her at the cottage known as 'Marigold' and although they had no children of their own they adopted a son, Sandy, who thrived despite his unconventional upbringing. Edith enjoyed children and many of her nieces and nephews spent their summers with her where she taught them about nature and the universe.

In 1926 she moved to North Wales, where she had been educated at Penrhos College as a girl. Sadly, her husband died just before the move, but Edith went anyway, to the place where she could walk in the mountains. Here, she soon surrounded herself once more with like-minded people. She formed an 'Anthroposophical Circle' and her house was always filled with visitors, much as Winckley Square had been in the days of the suffragette movement. She bathed in the sea every morning, both summer and winter, and took her visitors on long fell-walking expeditions through the mountains. Edith also became interested in Steiner's educational beliefs and visited New York to see one of his schools.

Even when she was past seventy she rose every morning at 4.00 a.m. to meditate. But old age and Parkinson's disease were events that Edith Rigby found it impossible to campaign against and she eventually died at her house near Llandudno in 1948.

James Kenyon and Sagar Mitchell

1866-1952 and 1851-1925

Their films captured a record of local life

The discovery, in 1994, of 800 small spools of cellulose nitrate black-and-white film stored in metal drums in the cellar of a shop in Blackburn, revealed the everyday lives of a past generation, as well as some of the first films that told stories.

Workmen at 40 Northgate discovered the stash in the cellar and loaded it onto their lorry to take to the scrapyard at Mill Hill, but on their way they passed a video shop owned by Nigel Gregory, who advertised ciné film to video conversion, and they stopped off to ask him if he thought it was worth keeping. He contacted local optician and film historian Peter Worden, who realised how important the twenty-six hours of films could be and he stored them until the highly inflammable films were preserved and restored by the British Film Institute's National Film and Television Archive.

The films were the work of James Kenyon and Sagar Mitchell who had captured a unique record of life during Victorian and Edwardian times. They had filmed workers, football matches, holidaymakers, celebrations and much more to give a glimpse of a lifestyle and people that were in danger of being forgotten.

James Kenyon was born on 26 May 1850. The census of 1881 records him as living at 12 Plymouth Street in Blackburn and working as a cotton spinner. In 1872 he married Elizabeth Fell and when her uncle died he inherited his cabinet making and furniture business at 21 King Street, although he worked mainly manufacturing penny-in-the-slot machines. Sagar Mitchell was also born in Blackburn sixteen years later on 28 October 1866 and worked in the family photographic business on Northgate.

The two men founded the firm of Mitchell and Kenyon in 1897 to produce films. They had invented a new way of making films that eliminated the noise and the erratic images that had previously spoiled viewing. An article in the *Blackburn Times* of 27 November 1897 reports on a demonstration of their new Norden apparatus, when they showed *Blackburn Market on a Saturday Afternoon*.

By 1899 they were using Norden as a trading name and had premises at 22 Clayton Street called the Norden Film Works where they also had an outdoor studio. It was in April of that year that they were commissioned by the owner of a travelling fairground, George Green, to film local people streaming out of the mills and factories at the end of the day. The films were shown at the Easter Fair and this idea continued in many other towns with either themselves or the showman handing out leaflets inviting people to come and see themselves on the screen as others saw them.

As well as recording film of everyday life Mitchell and Kenyon began to make fictional stories, including one of their most successful films which recreated scenes from the Boer War and was filmed up on the Yellow Hills at Billinge near Blackburn. Other titles included *The Tramps Surprise*, *Kidnapping by Indians*, *The Tramps and the Artist*, and, in 1904, *Black Diamonds*, which was the story of a coalminer's life and used film of a real coalmine combined the fictional events. They also made comedy films, including *Diving Lucy* in 1903,which included footage shot in Blackburn's Queen's Park, showing a woman's legs sticking up out of the lake and rescuers setting up a plank for a policeman, who discovers it is a trick when he is tipped into the water. It was a huge success and was also shown in France and the USA where it was acclaimed as 'the hit British comedy of the year'.

There were records of important national events too, which were shown countrywide. Both men were up by four in the morning to film the funeral of Queen Victoria in 1902, with Sagar Mitchell at Hyde Park Corner and James Kenyon at Windsor. And in 1905 they were present to film the unveiling of Queen Victoria's statue on Blackburn Boulevard.

They continued making films together until 1913. James Kenyon retired to Southport in 1915, but only lived there for six years before returning to Blackburn to live at 28 Granville Road, where he died on 6 February 1925 at the age of seventy-four. He was buried in Blackburn Cemetery.

The report of James Kenyon's death in the local paper described him as a cinematograph pioneer and reminded readers that he had almost died some years earlier in November 1901 when, having gone to Sunderland to film a great storm, he almost drowned. He had his camera on a slope near the old North Pier and was turning the handle to film the sea when a huge wave hit the shore, forcing him to abandon his camera and film and run for his life.

The article also records that he filmed the Crown Prince of Siam at Liverpool, and the late King Edward and Queen Alexandra. The journalist also laments that 'the advent of the Americans in the "movie" trade caused cinematography to become an unprofitable business for small firms', and that three years previously James Kenyon and Sagar Mitchell had dissolved their partnership. It is also interesting to read that he left a daughter, married to a Mr G. H. Roberts, who was a South African representative for Lever Brothers Ltd.

Sagar Mitchell continued to run his photographic shop in Northgate where he specialised in portrait photography, but he also carried on making films. In 1931 he went up in an aeroplane to film the Lancashire coast between Liverpool and Southport, though the results were not as good as he hoped owing to the wind that prevented the plane from being held steady. Recalling the event to the *Blackburn Times* he said, "We were perched on a couple of ordinary bicycle seats without any fuselage about us. After a rough trip, during which we found ourselves in danger of being shot-up while flying over a rifle range, we made a rather bumpy landing in the sand." And, no stranger to danger, on another occasion he was strapped to the front of a specially chartered steam engine to film the railway scenery between Lakeside and Ulverston, a trip which almost ended in disaster, as they narrowly missed a head-on collision with an express train coming in the other direction.

Sagar Mitchell died at the age of eighty-five and his obituary in the *Blackburn Times* describes him as an aerial photo pioneer and probably the first Blackburn man to fly. It also records that he was one of the first people in Blackburn to own a motorcar. He was buried at Mellor in the parish churchyard.

Emmaline Pankhurst

1858-1928

The Manchester suffragette

Emmaline Pankhurst who is probably the best known of the suffragettes was born in Manchester in 1858; she was the daughter of businessman Robert Goulden and his wife Sophia Crane. Her father
campaigned against both the Corn Laws and slavery and her mother
was an ardent feminist who took her young daughter with her to
women's suffrage meetings in the 1870s.

Emmaline was well educated, having been sent to school in
Manchester and to a finishing school in Paris at the age of fifteen.
When she returned to Manchester in 1878, she met Richard
Pankhurst, who was a lawyer and a socialist who supported women's
right to have the vote, and though he was forty-four and she was only
twenty her father gave her permission to marry him. They had four
children: Christabel, Sylvia, Frank and Adela.

In 1889 Richard and Emmaline helped form the pressure group,
the Women's Franchise League. The government of the day advised
that if women wanted to vote they should prove themselves worthy
by serving the community, though mostly in unpaid roles. So in 1895
Emmaline became a Poor Law Guardian, which involved visits to the
workhouse where she was deeply shocked by the conditions she
found, discovering that the men in charge were more concerned with
finance and saving money than alleviating suffering.

She found elderly people having to sit on backless benches and
insisted that they were provided with proper chairs. And in her autobiography *My Own Story* she recalls how she was horrified to see little
girls of around seven or eight years on their knees scrubbing the cold
stones of the long corridors. These little girls were clothed, both
summer and winter, in thin cotton frocks and at night they wore nothing at all, as night dresses were considered too good for paupers. And
the fact that bronchitis was rife had not alerted the guardians to
change the fashion of their clothes. She also questioned the practice
of giving young mothers with two-week-old babies the choice of stay-
ing in the workhouse to scrub floors or leaving with their child to
make their own living. What she saw not only shocked and horrified
her, but reinforced her belief that votes for women was the only way
forward to improve the social conditions of the country.

Emmaline and her husband were both members of the Labour Party and Richard stood as a parliamentary candidate until he died of a perforated ulcer in 1898.

By 1903 Emmaline had become disenchanted with the existing women's political organisations and on October 10, 1903 she invited a number of women to her house in Nelson Street, Manchester to create a new organisation. They called themselves the Women's Social and Political Union with "Deeds, not Words" as their motto.

By this time the media were losing interest in women's struggle for the vote and Emmaline decided that the previous quiet campaigning was having little effect and that it was time to make people take notice by using different methods to draw attention to the cause. Their campaign was to include window breaking, stone throwing, fighting and arson.

On 12 May 1905 a bill to give women the vote was 'talked out' by MPs; this happens if MPs are still debating a bill when the parliament adjourns. Comments included one from an unnamed MP who said that men and women differed mentally with women having little sense of proportion and that it would not be safe to give them the vote.

On 13 October 1905, her daughter, Christabel Pankhurst and Annie Kenny went to a meeting in London where MP Sir Edward Grey was speaking. They heckled him, calling out, "Will the Liberal Government give votes to women?" When they refused to be quiet they were evicted, kicking and spitting, from the meeting by the police who arrested them and charged them with assault. They were found guilty and fined five shillings each, which they refused to pay and were sent to prison. They weren't the first women to go to prison for their cause but they were the first to resort to violence; and in 1906 the term 'suffragettes' was first used by the *Daily Mail* as a derogatory label for women in the WSPU.

The same year a deputation of women travelled to Downing Street to meet the Prime Minister, Campbell-Bannerman to plead their right to the vote. He told them that they must be patient but addressing a meeting in Trafalgar Square Emmaline Pankhurst told the crowd of six hundred, "We have been patient too long. We will be patient no longer."

A split grew between those who favoured lawful persuasion and the Pankhurst family and their supporters. In 1907 Emmaline moved to London to be with her two elder daughters and to support the militant struggle. For the next seven years she was in and out of prison and went on hunger strike ten times as women were arrested for their increasingly militant campaign for votes.

On 4 August 1914, the First World War began when England declared war on Germany and a few days later all the suffragettes were released from prison on the understanding that the WSPU stopped its militant activities and supported the war effort. With a £2,000 grant from the government, the organisation turned its attention to work for women and organised a demonstration in London demanding that women were allowed to do jobs traditionally associated with men.

The newspaper of the WSPU changed its name from *The Suffragette* to *Britannia* and gained a new slogan 'For King, For Country, For Freedom'. It attacked politicians and government for not doing enough to win the war.

In 1917 Emmaline and her daughter Christabel formed the Women's Party, which supported 'equal pay for equal work, equal marriage and divorce laws, the same rights over children for both parents, equality of rights and opportunities in public service, and a system of maternity benefits'. Though now they turned their backs on their earlier socialist beliefs and advocated the abolition of the trade unions.

After the war she spent several years in the USA and Canada, lecturing for the National Council for Combating Venereal Disease. On her return to the UK in 1925 she joined the Conservative Party and was a candidate for a seat in the East End of London. She died in 1928, having fallen out with her daughter Sylvia over politics and Sylvia's illegitimate baby son, both of whom she refused to see.

Although her name is associated with the fight for women's votes, Emmaline Pankhurst did much more for the rights and social status of women and it seems a shame that she became so inflexible in her old age that she could not be reconciled with her daughter and grandson.

Pit Brow Lasses

1842-1960

Women in a man's world

When people think of coalminers they probably visualise men with dirty faces and lamps strapped their heads, but women and children worked in coalmining too. The Coal Mines Act of 1842 prohibited them from working underground, but women, especially in the Wigan area, continued to toil on the surface, sorting coal, rather than going deep underground to extract it from the earth. They were known as Pit Brow Lasses and were proud of their occupation.

The Pit Brow Lasses worked in the open air. Their tasks were various and included stacking coal, pushing wagons from the coal shaft to the stock heap, sorting the mined coal as it passed them on 'screens'

The Pit Brow Lasses *(photograph courtesy of Billinge History/Heritage Society)*

into large and small lumps, and sieving the coal to sort the useable chunks from the dust and dirt.

On 4 August 1911 it was proposed that women should no longer be allowed to do this work as it was 'degrading and improper'. But in his book *Lancashire Stories*, Frank Hird records that 'the opposition of the Lasses has so far been triumphant'.

With a lower age of fifteen, most of the girls were young and single and they usually gave up the work when they married, though a small number of married women and widows also did the work and in Wigan there was a woman who worked at the pit brow all her life until she was over sixty.

They dressed in trousers with a flannel jacket and scarves which covered their heads, leaving only their faces exposed. However, they were required to wear a skirt over the trousers which was tucked up whilst working but let down to walk to and from the pit so that they were 'decently attired'.

The Pit Brow Lasses were proud of their jobs and had a reputation for being healthy with fresh complexions. And when you compare the job with the alternative of working all day in the dust laden air of the cotton mills there may have been some truth in it. The girls earned good money and when washed and dressed in their 'best' clothes were unrecognisable.

Yet women working in this industry were treated as curiosities, as it wasn't considered normal for women to work at what most people perceived as a man's job. The women were often photographed for picture postcards and these pictures were often staged to show how small the women were and yet how strong. They were also often portrayed as unfeminine, though some show the women in both work wear and their best clothes to draw a contrast between the two.

But when parliament threatened to outlaw the work, a group of Lancashire girls dressed in their working clothes and went to Westminster to prove that they were neither unhealthy nor unfeminine.

Joseph Briggs

1873-1938

Donated Tiffany Glass to the people of Accrington

Joseph Briggs was born at 3 Milnshaw Lane in Accrington on 11 December 1873. After leaving school in 1887 he became an apprentice engraver at Steiner's Calico Printing Works in Church, where his father was a foreman.

Three years later, at the age of seventeen, he decided to go to America. He sailed from Liverpool on 21 September aboard the SS *Servia*, arriving in New York nine days later. It is unclear what he did for the next couple of years, though it seems he spent some time travelling around with a friend called Seth Hathaway who was a Pony Express rider and worked in a Wild West show.

In 1893 he bumped into Louis Comfort Tiffany, the glass designer, outside his shop in New York and persuaded him to give him a job. He was employed at first as an errand boy and general handyman, but his

Joseph Briggs

obvious talent meant that he quickly rose from this role. When Tiffany saw some of the mosaics he had made with fragments of left over glass he realised that he was a talented designer and trained him in the making of stained-glass windows and mosaics.

In 1898 he married Elizabeth Jenkins. Within a couple of years they had two small children and returned to live in Accrington for around six months but then went back to New York where Joseph became the foreman and manager of the mosaic workshop at Tiffany Studios.

Under Joseph Briggs'

direction the company undertook three major commissions. In 1905 the Studio began work on a stained-glass fire curtain for the Mexico City Theatre. The design reproduced the view from the presidential palace, showing a lake, trees and snow-capped mountains in the distance. It was exhibited in New York before being shipped to Mexico City in 1911 and despite weighing twenty-seven tons it used a system of hydraulic pressure and counterbalances that allowed it to be raised or lowered in only seven seconds.

Tiffany Studios then went on to produce the *Dream Garden* mosaic, designed by artist Maxfield Parrish for the Curtis Publishing Company in Philadelphia, which was installed in 1915. The mosaic, measuring forty-nine feet wide and fifteen feet high, was made from over a million pieces of Favrile glass and each one was hand-fired to achieve a perfect match of the 260 colours used. The name 'Favrile' for his glass was chosen by Tiffany from an old Saxon word, fabrile, meaning 'hand wrought'. The main characteristic of the glass is its iridescence in shades of blue, green and gold.

This partnership between Tiffany Studios and Maxfield Parrish has been called "One of the major artistic collaborations in early 20th Century America". In 1998, *Dream Garden* was sold to a casino owner who planned to move it to Las Vegas, but the people of Pennsylvania protested and money was raised to buy it back and it is now permanently installed in its rightful home in the Curtis Center lobby.

Joseph Briggs also worked on the St Louis Cathedral in Missouri, which was decorated with tiles and mosaics in the traditional Italian style.

In 1906, Joseph Briggs became an American citizen and built a house at Wood-Ridge in New Jersey. It was filled with Tiffany windows, tiles and mosaics and here he and his wife would give dinner parties for prospective clients.

When Louis Comfort Tiffany retired in 1919, Joseph was appointed as the managing director of Tiffany Studios.

Although the name Tiffany is now associated with lamps, it is said that Tiffany was embarrassed by them, and that they were only produced to use up the glass left over from the production of stained-glass windows. These were mainly for churches, though the firm was commissioned to make windows for private houses, banks, libraries and other public buildings all over the USA.

Towards the end of Tiffany's life, however, his glass became less popular. A combination of the Depression and the fashion for more modern windows in churches proved a downturn in fortune for the company. The manufacture of Favrile glass was discontinued around 1928 and in 1932 Tiffany Studios filed for bankruptcy.

When Louis Comfort Tiffany died in 1933, the direction of the Tiffany Studios was given to Joseph Briggs, through a clause in his will which said that the Tiffany Studio should close "when Mr. Briggs becomes too old or infirm to give them his personal direction and ensure the perpetuation of the Tiffany ideals in design and execution of stained-glass". But all that was left for Joseph Briggs to do was to dispose of Tiffany Studios' assets and a total of five cases of glass, containing 140 pieces of intricate and beautifully coloured glassware, was shipped to his home town as a gift to the people of Accrington. These are now on display at the Haworth Art Gallery in Accrington and comprise the largest public collection of glassware of its type in Europe and the largest collection of Favrile glass outside the USA.

Joseph Briggs died on 30 March 1938, in a New York hospital at the age of sixty-four.

Wallace Hartley

1878-1912

His band played on as the *Titanic* sank

Wallace Hartley is best remembered as the bandmaster who played 'Nearer My God To Thee' as the *Titanic* sank. Whether this particular hymn was actually played isn't clear, but it was the bravery of Hartley and his band of musicians in continuing to play music that went some way to preventing a mass panic and a stampede for the lifeboats on that night and could have saved many lives.

Wallace Henry Hartley was born on 2 June 1878 at 92 Greenfield Road in Colne. His parents, Albion and Elizabeth Hartley were textile workers and he had an elder sister Mary Ellen and a younger sister Lizzie. A younger brother died in infancy.

The family were all musical. His father was the choirmaster at the Bethal Chapel in Colne and young Wallace sang in the choir there. He was also a very talented violinist. His father encouraged him to take extra music lessons after school, and by the age of fifteen he was giving solo performances.

When he left school Wallace Hartley went to work in a local bank, the Craven and Union, as a clerk and stayed there until he moved with the family to Huddersfield in 1895. Here, he joined the Huddersfield Philharmonic Orchestra where he played the violin – although he continued to work as a clerk in a bank during the day.

In 1903, he eventually managed to leave banking to pursue a career in music and moved to the seaside town of Bridlington where he played First Violin in the Bridlington Municipal Orchestra.

In 1909, he began his career as a musician on board the Cunard liners that sailed between the UK and USA. He first joined the *Lucania*, though his first voyage turned out to be the ship's last as she was laid up by Cunard after returning from New York. Next he joined the *Lusitania*, playing the second violin in the ship's five-man band, and in October 1910 he was promoted to the position of bandmaster on board the *Mauretania*, which was the best and fastest ship afloat at the time, and the first passenger vessel to be fitted with the new steam turbine engine, developed by engineer Charles Parsons. The *Mauretania* was a very prestigious ship, having taken the Blue Riband for the fastest western crossing of the Atlantic the year before in 1909, a record she held for twenty years. But in December 1911 the

The memorial to Wallace Hartley at Colne

ship broke free from her moorings on the River Mersey and ran aground, damaging her hull and leaving Wallace Hartley unemployed whilst she was repaired.

During this time both Cunard and White Star Lines decided to employ the firm of musical agents C.E. & F.N. Black to supply the musicians for their ships. Whilst most of the same musicians were employed they were so on a lower rate of pay and could be sent by the firm to serve on any ship, rather than being assigned to just one. Although Wallace Hartley re-joined the repaired *Mauretania* for her 23 March sailing to New York, on his return he was told by Blacks that he was to be the bandmaster on the new White Star Lines ship *Titanic* when she sailed from Southampton in two days' time. He was reluctant at first, as he had just proposed to his fiancée, Maria Robinson, and was considering giving up working on the ships to be with her. But not only was this a promotion, it also meant a pay rise for the musician who was not highly paid and, hoping that the voyage would provide him with contacts for future work, he agreed to go.

On 10 April 1912, Wallace Hartley and his band played on the upper deck of the ship as the First Class passengers embarked. On board the ship he was in charge of two small orchestras – a quintet that played at evening dinner, after dinner concerts and Sunday

services, and a trio consisting of violin, cello and piano
that played in the reception
room outside the restaurant.
The *Titanic* made good
speed westwards across the
Atlantic towards New York
until there was a sighting of
ice around noon on Sunday
14 April. By this time
Wallace Hartley had crossed
the North Atlantic Ocean
over eighty times, so he
probably wasn't unduly
concerned, but shortly after
midnight, it became clear
that the ship was sinking
and passengers were
directed to the lifeboats.
Wallace Hartley assembled
all the musicians together to
play in the First Class
lounge. As people in life
jackets waited to board lifeboats, the band continued to
play as if nothing was amiss.
And when passengers were
moved out onto the Boat
Deck, Wallace Hartley and
his musicians moved
outside too, to continue
playing.

Wallace Hartley's grave in Colne cemetery

Many people believe that their playing helped to keep passengers
calm and allowed the lifeboats to be loaded in an orderly fashion and,
as the band kept playing, many passengers did not realise how serious the situation was.

At 2.20 a.m. on 15 April 1912 the *Titanic* sank and in the last wave
to engulf the decks all eight bandsmen were swept into the icy waters.
None was saved.

Two weeks later, Wallace Hartley's body was found floating in the
Atlantic Ocean by the cable ship *Mackay-Bennett.* At first recorded as

body number 224, his identity was soon apparent. He was still clothed in his bandsman's uniform of brown overcoat, green facings, black boots and green socks. His music box was still strapped to his body and amongst the items found in his pockets was a gold fountain pen with his initials on – W.H.H.

His body, perhaps ironically, packed in ice to preserve it, was returned to the UK aboard the SS *Arabic* and he was brought home to Colne to a hero's welcome. Over 40,000 people lined the streets of the small town to pay their respects at his funeral on 18 May. The procession, led by seven bands, made its way to the Bethel Chapel, where Wallace had sung in the choir as a boy, and was almost half a mile long. The congregation for the service totalled over a thousand, in a building designed only to hold seven hundred.

Wallace Hartley was buried in the small cemetery on the edge of Colne, in the family grave, as an orchestra played 'Nearer My God To Thee'; a page from Arthur Sullivan's setting of the hymn and a violin are carved into his gravestone, which reads: 'In Loving Memory of Wallace Henry, the beloved son of Albion and Elizabeth Hartley Formerly of Colne who lost his life in the SS *Titanic* Disaster on April 15th, 1912, aged 33 years and was interred on May 18th 1912.'

There is also a memorial to Wallace Hartley on the main street in Colne that was erected in 1915. The plaque records that it was 'Erected by voluntary contributions to commemorate the heroism of a native of this town.'

Thomas Clarkson and the Lytham Lifeboat Crew

1886

Heroes of the *Mexico* disaster

On the promenade at St Annes, in the floral gardens not far from the pier, is a statue of a lifeboatman looking out to sea. It is a memorial to the members of the St Annes lifeboat who were all drowned on the night of Thursday, 9 December 1886 whilst trying to rescue the crew of the *Mexico*. But all the crew of the *Mexico* were brought safely ashore thanks to Thomas Clarkson and his crew on board the Lytham lifeboat.

There was a storm on the evening of 9 December when the *Mexico*, a large barque from Hamburg, set sail from Liverpool to Guayaquil, Ecuador's largest city and main port. She became grounded on the Horsebank, a large sandbank in the estuary of the River Ribble between Southport and Lytham. Just before ten o'clock she signalled that she was in difficulties and the Lytham lifeboat, *Charles Biggs*, was launched in a moderate west-north-west gale with a very heavy sea. At this time the lifeboats had oars and sails, no engines, and as the crew struggled to row against the heavy swell the boat filled with water four or five times and three of the oars were broken.

The St Annes boat, *Laura Janet*, also set out, under sail, to attempt a rescue but she was quickly swept away. And the lifeboat from Southport, the *Eliza Fernley*, battled against the wind and the sea and managed to come within about twenty yards of the *Mexico*, which was breaking up. Two of her masts had already gone, and her crew, lashed to various parts of the vessel, were shouting wildly for help. But a huge wave struck the *Eliza Fernley* tipping her upside down and all her crew were washed into the raging sea. Three members of the crew managed to get out from under the upturned boat and clinging to the underside were eventually washed ashore, although one of the men later died in hospital. The other ten bodies from the Southport boat were washed ashore during the course of Friday morning.

However, the boat from Lytham managed to reach the *Mexico*, and plucked the captain and crew from the sinking vessel and brought all twelve men safely to shore. The lifeboat crew then went back into the

The lifeboat memorial at St Annes to those drowned in the *Mexico* disaster

raging sea to try to save the crew of the St Annes boat, but they were too late and all of the crew drowned that night.

The bravery of coxswain, Thomas Clarkson, was recognised by the Royal National Lifeboat Institute who awarded him the Silver Medal for the rescue.

A total of twenty-seven lifeboatmen died at sea in the *Mexico* disaster, and it was possibly the worst RNLI disaster on record. A fund was set up for the bereaved families and with contributions from Queen Victoria, the German Emperor and the Port of Hamburg, a total of £50,000 was raised.

The disaster prompted a local businessman, Sir Charles Macara, to found the Lifeboat Saturday Fund. The first event was held in 1891 in Manchester when 30,000 people attended and £5,500 was collected. The Fund continued for twenty years until it was taken over by the RNLI in 1910.

The wreck of the *Mexico* was later salvaged and sold to a firm in Preston for £45, where she was repaired before being moored off the pier as a tourist attraction. After two years she was sold again and sailed to the Falkland Islands before returning in 1889 and finally sinking in 1890 off the Scottish coast.

The St Annes lifeboat station was closed in 1925 and the Lytham lifeboat assumed responsibility for the area. In 1932 it was re-named

The new Lytham St Annes lifeboat station

Lytham St Annes. It celebrated its 150th Anniversary in 2001. Collection for the work of lifeboat crews, who are all volunteers, continues to this day and Lytham St Annes currently has two boats. One is an inflatable D-Class in-shore lifeboat kept at Lytham, but because of the silting up of the estuary of the River Ribble the larger sea-going lifeboat, a Mersey Class boat named *Her Majesty the Queen*, was moved back to St Annes in 1999 and is now housed in a purpose-built boathouse opened in August 2003.

L. S. Lowry

1887-1976

He painted matchstalk men and matchstalk cats and dogs

Lowry, whose name will be forever linked with the 'matchstalk' men that brought him such fame, was born Laurence Stephen Lowry on 1 November 1887 at Barret Street in Stretford, Manchester. His parents, Robert and Elizabeth, were said to be a little disappointed because they had been hoping for a girl and his mother never really regained her health after the birth.

He went to Victoria Park School during the week and to Bennett Street Sunday School where his mother, who was a piano teacher, played the organ. At the age of eleven the family moved to Pine Grove, Longsight.

He did not enjoy his schooldays and left without passing any exams, but from being a small boy he loved to draw. After he left school in 1903 he began work as a clerk at the Manchester Insurance Company and began to attend evening classes at the Manchester Municipal College of Art, where one of the teachers was the French painter Adolphe Velette.

His early drawings and paintings were very different from the matchstalk men and industrial scenes for which he is best remembered. At college he studied antique and freehand drawing, but soon it was his impressions of the streets he saw during his working day that he was painting in his individual style.

Lowry later worked as a rent collector for the Pall Mall Property Company and became very familiar with the terraced streets and mills around Manchester, which he used as inspiration for his art, often pausing to make quick sketches on scraps of paper from his pocket. "I'll always be grateful to rent collection. I've put many of the tenants in my pictures," he once said. It was a job he continued until he retired in 1952, and though the firm was very supportive of Lowry's art and allowed him time off to attend exhibitions he kept quiet about his day job as he didn't want people to consider him a part-time painter.

In 1915 he attended the Salford School of Art in the evenings and it was here that he began to experiment with his 'matchstalk' men. In 1918 he studied the life classes at Manchester Academy of Fine Art

L.S. Lowry sketching *(photograph courtesy of The Lowry)*

and had his first exhibition at Manchester Art Gallery the following year.

In 1909 the family had moved to Pendlebury because of financial problems and when his father died in 1932, he left debts and Lowry's bedridden mother for whom he cared until her death. She died in 1939, just as his work was beginning to be recognised. He had been devoted to her and grieved her loss for the rest of his life.

"She didn't understand my paintings, but she understood me – and that was enough," he said.

He exhibited paintings in Manchester, London and Paris and during the Second World War was an official war artist, recording scenes of bombed out Manchester that he witnessed during his working day. He also spent his holidays at Berwick on the north east coast where he painted seascapes.

In 1948 he moved to Mottram in Cheshire after his landlord repossessed his house in Pendlebury. Lowry was a loner who avoided a social life and was sufficient to himself. His art was his life and his work was different from anything that had been painted before. He was influenced by no-one. Some praised his work whilst others criticised it as amateurish and childlike.

But during the 1960s, recognition of his talent grew. In 1961 he was awarded an Honorary Doctor of Letters at Manchester University and in 1962 he was elected as a member of the Royal Academy of Arts. In 1964 the Prime Minister, Harold Wilson, used his painting *The Pond* as his official Christmas card. In 1965 he was made a Freeman of the city of Salford and in 1967 his painting *Coming Out Of School* was used on a postage stamp.

He died on 23 February 1976 at Woods Hospital, Glossop aged eighty-eight, just months before a retrospective exhibition of his work opened at the Royal Academy. He was buried at Chorlton Southern Cemetery next to his parents.

As with many artists though, it wasn't until after his death that his work was fully appreciated. His painting *Going To The Match* sold at auction to the Football Association for £1.9 million in 1999.

Lowry was also the inspiration for the song 'Matchstalk Men', which was a hit for Brian and Michael shortly after his death.

In April 2000 The Lowry, named after the artist, was opened at Salford Quays. Along with two theatres and gallery space for contemporary exhibitions, it houses a permanent exhibition of L.S. Lowry's paintings; these were formerly displayed at Salford Museum and Art Gallery, which had collected his work since 1936.

Lowry died without any family and left his estate to a girl called Carol Lowry who had written to him in 1957 asking for advice on how to become an artist. He went to visit her and they became friends, but she had no idea that she was his heir until after his death.

Richmal Crompton

1890-1969

Creator of 'Just William'

Richmal Crompton Lamburn was born near Bury on 15 November 1890 and is probably best known as the author of the *Just William* books.

She was the second child of the three children born to Reverend Edward John Sewell Lamburn and his wife Clara, whose maiden name was Crompton. Richmal used her middle name of Crompton as her pen name and her unusual first name was a tradition of her mother's family. She had an elder sister Gwen and a brother called Jack, whose escapades provided inspiration for the *William* stories and who later became a novelist himself.

She was educated at St Elphin's in Warrington, which was a boarding school for daughters of the clergy, and then won a scholarship to study for a degree at the Royal Holloway College in Surrey. Afterwards she returned to the school – now re-located in Derbyshire after the original building was condemned – as the classics mistress to fulfil her promise to return and teach there.

In 1915 her father died suddenly after going into hospital for a minor operation. Her mother moved to London to live with Gwen and her husband, Thomas Disher. Jack was in Rhodesia, serving in the mounted police and was unable to return home because of the outbreak of the First World War, and so Richmal, feeling rather isolated, decided to move south to be near her family.

She went to teach at Bromley High School in 1915 and her mother moved in with her. It was at this time that her first stories were published in *Home Magazine*. But because she was worried that teachers weren't allowed a second job and wasn't sure whether her writing counted as such, she used the name Richmal Crompton.

In 1923 Richmal became ill with what her mother thought was flu, but she had contracted polio and although she recovered she lost the use of her right leg. She returned to teaching, but struggled as it became too physically arduous for her and eventually she gave it up to concentrate on her writing.

What's less well-known is that as well as writing the *William* stories, Richmal Crompton also wrote a total of forty-one books for adults, including *The Innermost Room*, *The Hidden Light*, *Millicent*

Dorrington, The Four Graces, Blue Flames, Portrait of a Family, The Odyssey of Euphemia Tracy and *The Inheritor*. Many of them were family sagas – and in fact the *William* books were originally aimed at an adult market and were published in *Home Magazine* and *Happy Mag*. Later, twelve of the stories were collected into a book and published by George Newnes in 1922. They were given the title *Just William* and marketed as children's stories. Though like many so-called 'crossover' novels they work on two levels, with the basic story being taken at face value by younger readers whilst also containing a more adult sub-text with references to the classical and cultural that most children would not understand.

Richmal Crompton died on 11 January 1969, after a heart attack at her home in Kent. She was still writing, even though her health wasn't good and her niece, Richmal Ashbee, helped to complete her last book *William the Superman* after her death.

By this time there were a total of thirty-eight *William* titles and by 1977 over nine million copies had been sold all over the world, both in English and in translation. Since then *William* has graduated onto television and the scrapes and antics of this scruffy little boy are still loved by many.

Eva Turner

1892-1990

Renowned opera singer

The opera singer Eva Turner was born in Oldham on 10 March 1892. Her father was an engineer at the Broadway Mill on Goddard Street and Eva was a pupil at Werneth Council School until the family moved to live in Bristol when she was nine.

Although she had always been musical and had taken piano lessons since her seventh birthday, it was in Bristol that she saw a performance by the Carl Rosa Opera Company and became interested in a career as a singer. By the age of eleven she was having singing lessons with Dan Rootham, who also tutored Dame Clara Butt, which would make her dream come true. And at thirteen she sang a solo in a Bristol church.

In 1911 she was enrolled at the London Royal Academy of Music where she studied for three years. She then joined the Carl Rosa Opera Company where she first sang in the chorus before being given some small solo parts. She made her solo debut singing the role of the page in *Tannhauser*. She was paid half a crown, which she put in her post office savings account.

By 1921 she had sung all over the country with the company in various roles and was described as gifted and promising. Then, in 1924, Ettore Panizza heard her sing in a performance of *Madame Butterfly* and asked to meet her backstage, where he offered her an audition to perform with the La Scala Company. She went to Milan to sing for Arturo Toscanini and was offered a contract there and then.

She spent the next four months learning Italian and on 16 November 1924 she sang the part of Freia in *Das Rheingold*. She was well received and though the auburn-haired Eva was only of a small stature her soprano voice was described as 'full volume with a brilliant attack at the top of the range'.

Soon she was singing major roles and toured Germany, South America and the United States before coming to Covent Garden, in London, where she sang in *Aida*. Though she was better known on the Continent than she was at home, she was Britain's first international opera star. In 1926 she made headlines throughout Italy for her performance in Puccini's new opera *Turandot*. She was offered a contract with the Teatro Regio of Turin and bought a small villa on the shores of Lake Lugano, where she enjoyed swimming in her spare time.

In June 1928, Eva sang *Turandot* at Covent Garden and received a standing ovation. It is for singing this opera that she is best known, with her singing being applauded for its strength and emotion. And in November the same year she sang for the first time in the USA, with the Chicago Civic Opera, as *Aida*, to much acclaim.

Her voice lost some of its power and stability by the late 1930s and she officially retired from singing in 1948, at the age of fifty, after a final performance of *Turandot* at Covent Garden.

Eva Turner *(photograph courtesy of Oldham Local Studies and Archives)*

In August of that year she sailed on the Queen Mary to New York and took up the post of Visiting Professor of Voice at Oklahoma University. She went for nine months and stayed for ten years.

After this she returned to London in 1959 and became Professor of Singing at the Royal Academy of Music, where she worked until she was in her eighties, teaching singing and judging competitions; she always demanded a high level of work and commitment from her students.

In 1962 she was made a Dame of the British Empire. In 1979 she was awarded an honorary doctorate of music by Manchester University.

She died on 16 June 1990, at the age of ninety-eight. She is buried in the churchyard at Standish parish church as her father came from Wigan.

Gracie Fields

1898-1979

'Our Gracie'

Born Grace Stansfield on 9 January 1898 above her grandmother 'Chip Sarah's' chip shop on Molesworth Street in Rochdale, it is as Gracie Fields, or simply Our Gracie that she is remembered. Her parents were Fred and Jenny Stansfield and she had two sisters, Edie and Betty and a brother. She attended Rochdale parish church school, later working as a half-timer in a cotton mill until leaving on 11 February, 1910 to go on the stage. She was twelve years old and her mother, Jenny, was keen that her daughter should have the career in the theatre that she had wanted so much for herself and been denied.

But there wasn't much glamour to begin with in the early days as Gracie toured with juvenile troupes. It wasn't until she met Archie Pitt and performed the review *Yes, I Think So* with him in 1915 that her real charisma as a singer and actress, as well as comedian, began to emerge. Other successful reviews followed and the couple married eight years later, in 1923, although he was much older than she was and many people believed it was for power rather than love that he proposed.

In 1925 another review, *Mr Tower of London*, was performed at London's Alhambra Theatre. It was a great success and the show toured across the country for nine years – making Gracie and Archie Pitt not only famous, but rich as well. Gracie topped the bill wherever they went and sang to packed theatres. She had a charming soprano singing voice and Eva Turner tried to persuade her to sing some opera, but she preferred to sing in her own unique style and make the audience laugh with such classics as 'The Biggest Aspidistra in the World', delivered in Lancashire dialect.

In 1931 she made the film *Sally In Our Alley*, featuring the song 'Sally' that became so inextricably associated with her name, though it's said that she eventually grew to loathe it.

Gracie made fifteen more films, though she said that she did not enjoy the work and much preferred playing to a live audience, where she could interact and manipulate the responses of those who had come to hear her. In 1937 she was not only awarded the freedom of Rochdale, but was invited to Hollywood, to publicise her contract with Twentieth Century Fox. She was now at the height of her popu-

larity and her career, but she also worked hard for charity and in 1938 she received the Order of Officer Sister of St John of Jerusalem, as well as the CBE from King George VI for her contribution to the entertainment industry.

Gracie toured through North America, including Canada and on to South Africa to great acclaim. But after making the film *Shipyard Sally* in 1939 she became ill and was diagnosed with cervical cancer. The public were devastated and she was deluged

Gracie Fields *(photograph courtesy of Rochdale Local Studies Library)*

with over 250,000 letters and telegrams from all over the world, wishing her well.

She underwent a hysterectomy, leaving her unable to have children, and then travelled to the house she had bought in 1933 on the island of Capri to convalesce – accompanied by her friend Mary Davey and film director, Monty Banks to whom she had become close.

But 1939 was also the start of the Second World War and, although not in the best of health, Gracie travelled with Arthur Askey to entertain the British Expeditionary Force troops in France. In 1940, following her divorce from Archie Pitt, she married Monty Banks in Los Angeles, but as Monty was Italian and Italy joined the war against the Allies that year, the couple did not return to Britain, where her new husband could have been imprisoned, but accepted an offer to tour Canada and America.

The decision lost Gracie much of her popularity. The press accused her of being a traitor and running away from the war, even though her work raised many thousands of pounds for the war effort. She visited the UK in both 1941 and 1943 to give concerts in factories and works canteens, performing 'Sing As We Go' to keep up the morale of the mostly women workers.

After the war, in 1948, she sang at the London Palladium. Unsure of her welcome she sang 'Take Me To Your Heart Again' and received a standing ovation. But her happiness was spoiled just two years later when Monty died from a heart attack, and even though she continued to perform in the theatre and make records, she began to spend more time on Capri where the couple had enjoyed many happy times.

It was here that she met Boris Alperovici, supposedly when he came to repair her broken gramophone, and she married him in February 1952 on the island. They were to be married for twenty-five years until her death. Following the marriage Gracie continued to sing and entertain, appearing in variety shows in the UK as well as making tours in Canada and Australia.

In her seventies she was a guest on *Stars on Sunday* in 1969, and in 1975 she again returned to Britain to make what was to be her last album – *The Golden Years of Gracie Fields*.

In September 1978 she opened a new theatre in her home town of Rochdale, which was named in her honour. And that same year she sang 'Sally' for the last time at the Royal Variety Performance. It was to be her last performance.

The following February she was made a Dame and received her award from the late Queen Mother at Buckingham Palace, but by July 1979 she was in hospital in Naples suffering from pneumonia – and although she returned home to Capri in the August she died on 27 September at the age of eighty-one.

She is buried near her home on the Isle of Capri, but lives on in the hearts and minds of everyone, both as a legend and a Lancastrian – the millgirl who made it to the big time.

Helen Bradley

1900-1979

A great British artist

Helen Layfield Bradley was born on 20 November 1900 at 58 High Street in Lees near Oldham. In 1913 she won the John Platt scholarship to Oldham Art School, where she studied embroidery and jewellery making. But the First World War and her parents' doubts got in the way of her dream to be an artist and in 1926 she married the painter and textile designer Thomas Bradley and became an ordinary wife and mother. Tom worked as a designer at John Lewis on Oxford Street in London, and whilst living in the capital Helen took the opportunity to visit art galleries where she was influenced by Mogul and Persian art which used pictures to tell stories.

When she was sixty-five, and she and Tom had retired to Cartmel, she began to write about her Edwardian childhood for her grandchildren and she illustrated her stories with lively paintings to show them what life had been like when she was young. Each picture helped to tell the story and was full of action and vibrant colour, painted in a flat style with no roundness or shadows.

The paintings feature herself and her family as well as people she knew well. Besides her mother, her grandmother, her three maiden aunts, herself with her brother George and their dogs Gyp and Barney, she painted family friends such as Mr Taylor, the bank manager, and Miss Carter, who was a friend of her aunts. In fact if you look at any of her paintings you will probably see a figure in a pink dress, and this is Miss Carter. She is said to be the first figure that Helen painted and has been included in her pictures ever since.

Her work was first exhibited by the Saddleworth Art Society in 1965, followed in 1966 by an exhibition in London. People loved her work. It also became very popular in the United States and an exhibition at the Carter Gallery in Los Angeles followed in 1968.

In 1971, Jonathan Cape published her first book called *And Miss Carter Wore Pink*, in which she describes her life in both words and pictures, with images of trips to the coast, market days, fairgrounds to funerals, bread baking day, the races and carol singing in the snow.

It was a great success and three more books followed: *Miss Carter Came With Us*, which is a record of Lancashire life throughout 1908 and includes a suffragette meeting where Miss Carter fainted; "*In the*

Helen Bradley © *Helen Bradley Prints Ltd.*
www.helenbradley.co.uk

Beginning" said Great Aunt Jane, which recalls the Tuesday afternoons Helen spent listening to her aunt's stories about God, who polished the sun with Brasso and left on the tap in Manchester making it rain; and finally *The Queen Who Came to Tea*, which records the day King Edward and Queen Alexandra rode through the streets of Manchester when her Aunt Mary told her that Queen Alexandra had come to tea after the children had gone to bed and had learned the secret of making a proper Yorkshire pudding.

The books were all translated into German, French, Dutch and Japanese and a special edition was produced for the USA. Sadly they are out of print now, but are sought after by eager collectors.

Following this success, people began to ask for prints of her work and thirty signed Limited Edition prints, as well as three unsigned Limited Edition prints and eleven open edition prints were produced for sale, one of which is shown on the facing page. During the 1970s Helen became a celebrity and appeared on a television chat show with Russell Harty, on 'Pebble Mill at One' and as a guest on 'Desert Island Discs'.

She is now recognised as a great modern British artist and her paintings continue to grow in popularity and value, with original paintings now selling for many thousands of pounds. In 2005, Gallery Oldham bought her painting *A Special Treat* for their permanent collection. The picture shows Helen and her brother George being taken to see the colliery on their way home from Hollinwood Market in 1908.

Helen Bradley was awarded the MBE for services to the arts, but she died on 19 July 1979 just before she was due to receive her award from the Queen.

Family in Spring Lane © *Helen Bradley Prints Ltd. www.helenbradley.co.uk*

The print shown above is one of ten 'unlimited prints' listed on the www.helenbradley.co.uk/prints/ website with the accompanying description:

It was our last walk along Spring Lane before setting off for Blackpool the next morning. Grandma, the Aunts and Miss Carter (who wore Pink) called for us and as they walked along talking about all the little things they had to do before the cabs came the next morning, Willie and Annie Murgatroyd came running up to George and I, Annie saying that they would see us at the station the next morning as they were going to their Auntie's at Blackpool.

"What's the matter with Willie," said Grandma.

"He's got the mumps," shouted Annie.

"Oh dear me," said Mother, "that's the last straw. Children, put your hankies to your noses."

"I've never had the mumps," said Miss Carter, "and look, Mr. Taylor (the Bank Manager) is coming. Let us all turn back quickly." And the year was 1908.

Thora Hird

1911-2003

Talented actress

Thora Hird was born in Morecambe on 28 May 1911. She was the youngest of three children although her sister, Olga, died in infancy. Thora made her stage debut when she was just eight weeks old in the arms of her mother who was an actress at the Royalty Theatre. Her father, James Henry Hird, was the theatre manager. But despite this early stage appearance her father did not want her to be an actress and she spent ten years behind the counter of the local Co-op before joining Morecambe Repertory Theatre in 1931.

For the next ten years, she acted in over five hundred plays until she was seen by George Formby who arranged for a casting director from Ealing Studios to see her. After a screen test she was taken on by the studio for £10 a week, which was ten times what she had been earning.

In 1941 she made her first screen appearance opposite Will Hay in *The Black Sheep* of Whitehall. She appeared in and made over a hundred films including *The Entertainer* with Laurence Olivier and Shirley Ann Field, which was filmed in Morecambe. And although she didn't receive leading roles – mainly playing maids or landladies – and wasn't known for her beauty, she soon gained a solid reputation as a talented actress.

She also began to work in television and played the mother-in-law in *A Kind of Loving* in 1962. She became better known during the 1960s, appearing in *Meet The Wife*, shown on the BBC from 1963 to 1966, where she played her namesake Thora opposite Freddie Frinton as Fred Blacklock. In 1968 she appeared in the drama series *The First Lady*, where she played a crusading local councillor. In 1979 she appeared in *In Loving Memory*. During this time she was often working on a television series during the day and appearing in live theatre in the evening.

Her faith was also important to her and she was a well-known presenter of *Praise Be!* for seventeen years. She also enjoyed both gardening and travelling and went on pilgrimages to the Holy Land and Jordan during the 1990s.

Thora Hird was awarded the OBE in 1983 and became a Dame in 1993. She received an honorary doctorate from Lancaster University in 1989 and a Fellowship from the University of Central Lancashire in 2000. She published an autobiography *Scene and Hird* in 1976 and also wrote several other books about prayer. Some of her later television appearances included *Last of the Summer Wine*, where she played Edie Pegden and Alan Bennett's *Talking Heads* for which she won two BAFTA awards – one in 1989 for best TV actress for her performance in 'A Cream Cracker Under the Settee' and in 1998 for 'Waiting for the Telegram', when she portrayed a hundred-year-old resident in a nursing home. She won a third BAFTA in 1999 for *Lost for Words*, Deric Longden's autobiographical work about his mother's declining health.

She married James Scott on 3 May 1937 and he managed her career after he returned from the Second World War. Their daughter, Janette Scott, became a film actress and married the American singer Mel Tormé. James died in 1994 after nearly sixty years of marriage, but rather than retiring Thora Hird continued to do the job she loved almost to the end of her life, totalling nine decades in show business. Despite a bad fall which resulted in several weeks in hospital, angina, three hip operations and the arthritis that put her in a wheelchair, she continued to work. In fact it was in later life that she was offered some of her best parts and came into her own as a character actress.

Known for her bluntness, she had a tendency to speak her mind, but was also known for her kindness. In 1994 she was interviewed by Melvyn Bragg for the *South Bank Show*, but insisted that it was recorded at the Winter Gardens in Morecambe, where she became patron of the Friends of the Winter Gardens, who were campaigning to keep the theatre open.

She died on the 15 March 2003 at the age of ninety-one after suffering a stroke at Brinsworth House in London, which is a retirement home for actors.

Kathleen Ferrier

1912-1953

"Her voice and spirit gave hope and radiance to the world"

The famous singer, Kathleen Ferrier, was born at 53 Bank Terrace, Higher Walton, near Preston where her father was the headmaster of All Saints Church of England School. A plaque on the wall of the house, which was dedicated on 4 February 1956, reads: "Kathleen Ferrier CBE was born here on 22nd April 1912. A singer of international fame, her voice gave deep pleasure to multitudes. 1912-1953."

When Kathleen was eighteen months old the family moved to Blackburn when her father became head at St Paul's School and they lived at 57 Lynwood Road, near St Silas' School where Kathleen was educated between the ages of four and eleven, before moving on to the Blackburn Girls' High School.

She left school at the age of fourteen and trained as a telephone operator with the GPO on Darwen Street in Blackburn – the building which is now a pub named *The Postal Order*. Here she earned nineteen shillings a week and spent some of her wages on music lessons – first with Annie Chadwick and later with Thomas Duerden who was the organist and choirmaster at Blackburn Cathedral.

In 1934 she transferred to the Post Office in Blackpool and became involved with musical activities in Lytham St Annes. In 1935 at the age of twenty-three, she married and moved to Silloth in Cumbria where her husband worked for a bank. However, she and her husband did not live together again after he was 'called up' for the War and after eleven years the marriage was annulled.

Kathleen considered herself to be a pianist and won many prizes at local music festivals and it was at a music festival in 1937 that she was 'dared' by a friend to sing as well as play. She won the piano class with the highest marks ever recorded, but also won the contralto prize and the Rosebowl for the best singer at the festival.

During 1940 she studied music with Dr Hutchinson of Newcastle-upon-Tyne, but when Sir Malcolm Sargent heard her sing in Manchester in 1942 he encouraged her to travel to London to take lessons with Mr Roy Henderson.

Kathleen sang at Glyndebourne Opera in 1946 in *The Rape of Lucretia* by Benjamin Britten and in 1947 in *Orfeo* by Gluck. She sang at the first ever Edinburgh Festival; at Salzburg Festival; and in 1950 she toured the USA and Canada singing to capacity audiences before sailing home on the *Queen Elizabeth.*

Around that time she was interviewed at a Manchester hotel by Lancashire writer Joan Pomfret for the January 1949 issue of *Lancashire Life.* Joan describes her as "tall and graceful, with a charm of manner seldom encountered".

Singing and piano playing were not her only talents either. She loved to paint and always signed her pictures KK – an abbreviation for Klever Kaff!

But at the height of her career Kathleen became ill

Kathleen Ferrier *(photograph courtesy of The Ferrier Archive Blackburn Museum)*

and although she remained cheerful and did her utmost to continue with her singing almost until the end of her life, her battle with breast cancer was one she could not win.

When she was awarded the CBE in January 1953 she was too ill to attend the presentation at Buckingham Palace, and Gluck's *Orfeo* at Covent Garden was withdrawn after only two performances because of her ill-health.

Then living in Hampstead, Kathleen was treated at University College Hospital, where a memorial to her was unveiled in April 1958 inscribed: "Her voice and spirit gave hope and radiance to the world."

Kathleen died aged only forty-one on 8 October 1953. She was cremated at Golders Green and a memorial service was held in Southwark Cathedral on 24 November that same year.

In 1955, the Royal Philharmonic Society set up two Kathleen Ferrier Memorial Scholarships for singers aged between twenty-one and twenty-five years old, worth £300 each. Also the Kathleen Ferrier Cancer Research Fund was begun, raising over £50,000.

At her home town in Blackburn, a bronze bust of Kathleen by the Austrian sculptor Arthur J. Fleischmann was unveiled at a memorial concert in King George's Hall on 8 October 1954 – just a year after her death. The bust is now on display in Blackburn Museum and the museum also houses a collection of her scores and manuscripts and her Royal Philharmonic gold medal. In 1993, the Kathleen Ferrier Society was formed to provide an information service; to award bursaries to young singers; to collect memorabilia to be stored in Blackburn Museum; and to raise money for the Kathleen Ferrier Memorial Cancer Fund.

Fortunately there are still some remaining recordings of Kathleen Ferrier singing including her well-known rendition of 'Blow The Wind Southerly', the title used for a documentary programme made by the BBC in 1968, and other songs.

"She is irreplaceable," said Bruno Walter when he learned of her death. Within one decade she came from her quiet Lancashire home and conquered the world.

The Accrington Pals

1916

A battalion wiped out by 8.00 a.m.

At the outbreak of the First World War, Lord Kitchener appealed for volunteers to join the army and hundreds of local men in Lancashire, and all over the country, were promised that when they enlisted they would not be separated from their friends.

Just one month after the outbreak of war, the mayor of Accrington, Captain John Harwood, told the War Office that he would raise a complete battalion of men, and when recruitment began on 14 September 1914, 104 men were signed up in the first three hours. By 24 September the battalion was complete with 36 officers and over a thousand men in other ranks. And although there were recruits from other East Lancashire towns such as Blackburn, Burnley and Chorley, it became the 11th (Service) Battalion (Accrington) East Lancashire Regiment, later to be known as the Accrington Pals.

Accrington Pals on Ellison's Tenement, probably during the early recruiting campaign *(reproduced by permission of Lancashire County Library – South East Division)*

St John's Accrington has a memorial chapel to the Accrington Pals

The battalion trained and drilled around East Lancashire until the day when 16,000 people lined the streets to cheer them off as they travelled to join other troops. During 1915 the Pals trained at Caernarfon, Rugeley, Ripon and Salisbury Plain before sailing to Egypt in December. For over two months they guarded the Suez Canal. But in January 1916, the commanders-in-chief of the French and British armies agreed to mount a joint attack on the Western Front during the coming summer and the place chosen was along a wide front close to the River Somme. So, in early March 1916, the Pals sailed to France and went into the trenches to train for the battle.

In the early hours of the morning of 1 July, 1916, the first day of the infamous Battle of the Somme, following a seven-mile march from their camp at Warnimont Wood, the Accrington Pals advanced towards German trenches that were supposed to have been destroyed by a week of artillery bombardment. They were on the left flank of a pincer movement and their objective was to capture the hilltop fortress of Serre.

But the enemy troops were holed down in underground shelters built into the chalky landscape and had survived the week-long attack. As the Pals moved forward across No Man's Land they were overwhelmed by machine gun fire and, in less than thirty minutes, of the 720 Accrington Pals who fought on that day, 235 were dead and around 350 were wounded or went missing. The battalion of local Accrington men and boys was destroyed. The survivors were forced to withdraw and by eight o'clock in the morning the battle for Serre was over.

Back home the local paper, the *Accrington Observer & Times*, began to fill with the names and photographs of the killed and wounded. Most of the families in the town had lost a relative in the battle. At least 850 Pals died during that war. Many are buried in cemeteries in France and Belgium, but 320 have no known grave and are commemorated on seven memorials.

The infamous Battle of the Somme continued throughout 1916 until the winter put an end to the fighting and Serre remained in the possession of the Germans until February the following year. There were a total of over 600,000 British and French casualties, and German losses were high as well, although only a few miles of ground were won.

As well as the Cenotaph in Oak Hill Park there is a memorial chapel to the Accrington Pals in St John's Church and an annual service in memory of the Pals is held on the Sunday nearest to the 21 February. In 2004 a memorial was unveiled on Church Street, which commemorates the granting of the freedom of the Borough of Hyndburn to The Queen's Lancashire Regiment on 29 June 2002, but is dedicated to the memory of The Accrington Pals.

Eric Morecambe

1926-1984

Well-loved comedian

What better tribute could a Lancastrian give to the county of their birth than to change their name to that of the town where they were born?

Eric Morecambe was born John Eric Bartholomew on 14 May 1926 in Buxton Street in Morecambe. He was the only child of George and Sadie Bartholomew, and his mother, wanting him to be successful, paid for him to have dancing lessons that he hated, but which came in so useful when he teamed up with Ernie Wise.

As a child, Eric used to enter talent competitions and he entered one at Hoylake, on the Wirral, in 1939, where the prize was an audition with Jack Hylton the bandleader, and it was here that he first met Ernie who was to become the other half of the famous double act.

Three months later, Eric received a telegram from Jack Hylton, asking him to join a review called *Youth Takes a Bow* at the Nottingham Empire. Ernie Wise was also in the show and it was from here that they developed their act and went on to appear together in Liverpool and Glasgow.

But when he was eighteen, Eric was called up for National Service. He worked as a Bevin Boy, down a coal mine near Accrington. The work badly affected his health and may have been partly responsible for his later heart attacks and early death.

After the war, Eric met Ernie by chance on the street. They decided to team up again and soon their success began to grow as they worked both on stage and on radio, although their first television appearance in 1954 was savagely criticised and sapped the confidence of the young comedians.

Eric married Joan Bartlett in 1952 and they had a daughter, Gail, a son, Gary, and an adopted son Stephen.

After more success on the radio, he and Ernie worked on *Sunday Night at the London Palladium* and in 1961 were given their own television show. *The Morecambe and Wise Show* became a national institution – especially the 'Christmas Special', with famous guests from near and far clamouring to go along to be insulted. In fact the 1977 'Christmas Show' entered *The Guinness Book of Records* for having the largest British television audience of twenty-eight million viewers.

But in 1968 Eric suffered his first heart attack, forcing him to take

The statue of Eric Morecambe

time away from public life to recover. It was then that he enjoyed birdwatching and fishing.

Eric was a keen bird-watcher and the statue of him in Morecambe, by Graham Ibbeson and unveiled by the Queen in 1999, shows him in his well-known comic pose, but also depicts binoculars hanging around his neck.

He also enjoyed fishing, a pastime he had been intro-duced to by his father, who would take him fishing around Morecambe Bay when he was younger. He wrote a book called *Eric Morecambe on Fishing* (Pelham Books, 1984) and spent time fishing for trout on the River Test in Hamp-shire, though he never lost his love of eating cockles and mussels caught at Morecambe.

Eric's other passion was football, especially Luton Town Football Club, where he was a club director in 1970 and vice president in 1977.

Despite his public persona he was a perfectionist behind the scenes and worried constantly about the quality of his work, which added to his stress.

Eric and Ernie were awarded the OBE in 1976. But despite over-coming his health problems, and another heart attack in 1979, to return to a successful career in comedy, including energetic song and dance routines with Ernie and a punishing schedule of shows, Eric suffered another heart attack on 28 May 1984. This time it was fatal. He died soon after coming off the stage at a charity show in The Roses Theatre, Tewkesbury.

Eric's funeral was held at the church of St Nicholas in Harpenden and his ashes were scattered in the memorial garden. A comedian to the end, he had written to his friend Dickie Henderson saying: "I would like to be cremated, and my favourite music is 'Smoke Gets In Your Eyes'."

Fred Dibnah

1938-2004

A reputation built on felling chimneys

Famous for his oily overalls, flat cap and climbing tall chimneys it isn't often that someone achieves stardom for destroying things.

Fred Dibnah was born on 29 April 1938 in Bolton. He began work as a joiner, making coffins, and spent two years in the army as a chef during his National Service, but from being a small child he had been fascinated by the machinery of the Industrial Revolution.

He also had a fascination with steeplejacks and soon began working in this area. He enjoyed repairing and renovating buildings, but he also gained a reputation for felling chimneys, and thousands of people would gather to watch one of Fred's chimneys fall. Fred never used dynamite to bring chimneys down, preferring the method of removing part of the base of the chimney and propping it up with telegraph poles, then lighting a fire at the base. As the wood burnt away the chimney would become unstable and topple – almost always exactly in the place that Fred had planned.

In 1978, whilst he was working at the top of the town hall in Bolton, the local BBC news filmed a short item about him. This resulted in a request from television producer, Don Haworth, to make a half-hour programme about Fred's work as a steeplejack for a series about people with unusual occupations. However, the result became an hour long, award-winning, documentary called *Fred Dibnah – Steeplejack* which was shown in 1979.

This was just the start of Fred's career in the media and he went on to make many documentary programmes that were shown on the BBC including *Fred Dibnah's Industrial Age (1999)*, *Fred Dibnah's Magnificent Monuments (2000)*, *Fred Dibnah's Buildings of Britain (2002)* and *Fred Dibnah's The Age of Steam (2003)*.

People were fascinated, not only by his work but by his blunt northern charm, his unpolished Bolton accent and his ability to talk endlessly on the subjects that enthralled him. And many people who met him said that with Fred what you saw was the real thing; he was just the same, whether on television or in person.

The fame had its repercussions on his personal life though and he was divorced from two of his wives before marrying for the last time in 1998. Sheila, his third wife was twenty years his junior and a

Fred Dibnah

former Blackpool showgirl; perhaps a surprising choice for a man who always seemed to be coated in grease and either up a chimney or deep in an engine. But as his television fame proved, Fred was never short of charm.

But Fred's real passion was steam engines. He'd long had an ambition to restore a steam engine and, when a friend found one in a Welsh barn, Fred paid £170 for it and towed it home. The engine was originally owned by Flintshire County Council in North Wales and had been in use until the 1960s when it was sold for scrap. He named the engine *Betsy* after his mother and it took him twenty-five years to restore it, using traditional methods to make the spare parts for rebuilding.

Fred was diagnosed with cancer in 2001. He was later given chemotherapy but after his first course of treatment made him feel so ill he couldn't work, he stopped it. He was determined to finish the twelve-part series *Made In Britain* that he was filming for the BBC, which featured him travelling around the country on his restored steam engine *Betsy*. Shown in the spring of 2005, after his death, the programmes showed Fred investigating Britain's industrial heritage and his smiles and jokes belied his serious illness.

The programmes were a great tribute to his determination to highlight the importance of the country's industrial heritage and his determination not to let his illness stop him doing what he was so passionate about.

The programmes also featured him receiving his MBE, for services to heritage and broadcasting, at Buckingham Palace. He had taken *Betsy* along too, as well as his wife Sheila and his sons Jack and Roger. He had threatened to buy a new cap for the ceremony, but accepted the award in a morning suit, although his cap and driving attire were

Fred Dibnah with his MBE, photographed by Brian Elsey

close at hand, and he told waiting photographers that he was eager to get out of the 'penguin suit'.

He had plans to turn his back garden in Bolton into a working museum, though his efforts to sink a seventy-two foot mine shaft in his back garden were put on hold when the council came to inspect the hole. Fred's plans were to dig down to below the level of the River Tonge, then drive a tunnel to the river about a hundred feet long before installing the head gear and steam winding engine that had been waiting in the garden for over ten years. Perhaps to the relief of his neighbours this project was never fulfilled.

Fred died on 6 November 2004 in Bolton Hospice at the age of sixty-six. His funeral was held in Bolton on 16 November and his coffin was taken to Bolton parish church on a trailer pulled by *Betsy*, the black and green steam engine, driven by one of his sons.

Relishing a glass of Guinness at the end of the day, Fred will always be remembered as a Lancastrian who showed the rest of the country that oil and grime and engines were beautiful and worthy of preservation, and that the county should be proud of its industrial heritage.

Tom Finney

1922-

A skinny little lad that no-one wanted on their team

Tom Finney was born on 5 April 1922 in Preston. As a child he lived just across the road from the football ground, but being only small found that he was always the last to be picked for childhood games. Like many boys, he had dreams of becoming a footballer, but an infected gland in his neck at the age of six kept him a frequent visitor to the hospital until it was removed at the age of fourteen and his father, Alf, insisted that he learn a proper trade and Tom became an apprentice plumber.

Yet he still continued his dream and applied to the club. He was four feet nine inches tall and weighed just five stones, but he was offered a contract to join the ground staff with a wage of two pounds ten shillings a week. As well as playing for the junior side he would have been cleaning boots and sweeping the terraces, but again his father said no. Not to be thwarted, Tom signed as an amateur in 1937 and played part-time. He was a versatile player and although he was naturally left footed he practised so that he could play on left wing, right wing as well as centre forward.

It was three years later in 1940 when he became a professional player. But it was during the Second World War and ordinary football matches were suspended. In 1942 Tom was called up to serve as a trooper with the Royal Armoured Corps as a tank driver and mechanic, but he managed to play some football on the wartime guest circuit, playing football by invitation for Newcastle, Southampton and Bolton. When he was posted overseas to Egypt he also managed to keep up his football and played in a Force's side named The Wanderers and reputedly once played against Omar Sharif, who later became a film star. But it was a little different from Preston, with players having to remove mines from the pitch before kick-off.

Towards the end of the war he made his debut as an England player in a friendly game against Switzerland in Berne, though England lost on that occasion.

At the end of the war he had a quick discharge from the army, not because he was a famous footballer but because his plumbing skills were in high demand for rebuilding work. He rejoined Preston in 1946, plumbing by day and training in the evenings. And within four

This statue of Tom Finney, known as The Splash, is built from bronze and is one and a half times life size. It can be found at the entrance to the National Football Museum at Deepdale and was sculpted to depict a famous moment in his career.

weeks he was called up to play for England's 7-2 defeat of Northern Ireland.

Tom Finney played for England a total of seventy-six times and scored thirty goals. He played for Preston until he retired from the game in 1960, by which time he had made a total of 433 league appearances and scored a club record of 187 goals. But he did not enjoy the celebrity lifestyle that today's players do. At the same time as being a footballer he still ran his own part-time plumbing business in Preston and gained the nickname The Preston Plumber. Though in 1952, after a one all draw against Italy, Palermo offered him a signing on fee of £10,000 to play for them along with a weekly wage of over £100, a car and a villa. They also offered Preston a £30,000 transfer fee. Tom Finney declined the offer and remained at Preston, settling, instead, for a £2 a week pay rise.

In 1953 he was voted Footballer of the Year and in the same season won his only medal when Preston were beaten 3-2 by West Bromwich Albion in the FA Cup Final.

In 1957 he became the first person to win the Footballer of the Year for the second time. However, injuries forced his retirement in 1960, though he continued to run his business and later became a magistrate, chairman of his local health authority and President of Preston North End.

Well-known for his gentlemanly behaviour, Tom Finney was never booked during his years as a player. In 1961 he was awarded the OBE, followed by the CBE in 1992 and in 1998 he was knighted, becoming Sir Tom Finney.

Today, Preston North End is still an important part of Tom Finney's life. At well over eighty, he is still Club President and as well as his statue which can be found at Deepdale, a stand and the road running alongside the stadium are named in his honour. Not bad for a skinny little lad that no-one wanted on their team.

Josephine Cox

1938-

Best-selling author of regional sagas

Best selling novelist, Josephine Cox, was born in Blackburn during the Second World War and was brought up there until the age of fourteen. Her father worked as a groundsman at Ewood Park, Blackburn Rovers' football ground, and although she now lives in Oxfordshire, she makes regular visits to Blackburn to see family members who still live in the area and regards her roots as being firmly planted in Lancashire.

Her books are mostly set in and around the town and she uses the memories of her formative years, mingled with real places and street names to weave her popular tales about people and their lives.

Josephine has been telling stories since she was a child. She used to gather children around her on the bombsite at the bottom of Addison Street and tell them a story for a penny. And she didn't, as you might think, run off to the sweet shop afterwards, but she took the pennies home to her Mam to help feed the family of ten children.

She speaks affectionately of both her parents, but especially her Mam. Josephine tells her mother's story in her book *Angels Cry Sometimes*, which portrays the hard life she had. Josephine remembers her father, Barney Brindle, too, with much love.

"When he was sober he was loving, interesting and funny, but when he was drunk I didn't know him," she says.

It was partly because of this drunkenness that her mother made the brave decision to leave and take most of her children with her. They went to Bedfordshire where Josephine met Ken who was to become her husband just two years later. But life was never easy for Josephine. In the 70s Ken's haulage business fell victim to the recession and they lost their home. The council offered them a house that was so awful that at first Josephine admits she ran away from it. But with no other option she rolled up her sleeves and scrubbed it into a home where she, Ken and their two sons lived for seventeen years.

During this time Josephine returned to her studies and gained O-levels and A-levels and was offered a place as a mature student at Cambridge University – an offer that she rejected because it would have required her to live on campus away from her family.

The theme of looking disaster in the eye and overcoming it recurs

Josephine Cox © *Trevor Leighton*

again and again in her novels and no wonder it rings so true. Josephine's success was no overnight phenomenon. She hasn't had it easy and her stories tell us about life as it really is, much of it from first hand experience.

In fact it was another 'knock down' that was the catalyst for her career as a writer. Whilst working as a teacher, she was taken ill and hospitalised. A colleague told her that here was her chance to write that novel she had always been talking about. So, never shy of rising to a challenge, that's just what Josephine did. She wrote it in six weeks, though it took six more years of editing and polishing with the help of her publisher, whilst she was still teaching full time, before it was ready. But the same year her family secretly entered her for the *Superwoman of Great Britain Award*, which she won.

"When life knocks you down you have two choices," she says. "You can stay down or you can get up. Of course some people can't get up because it's out of their control, but I've always been lucky enough to get up and start again."

And recently that's just what Josephine had to do once more when, after more than forty years of happy marriage, Ken died suddenly.

She continues to produce stories and is the author of over forty best-selling north country sagas, and also writes under the name Jane Brindle. Each of her books is eagerly awaited by her fans worldwide and usually goes straight to the top ten in the book sales charts.

Barry Mason

1935-

The songwriter behind the hits

You may think that you've never heard of Barry Mason, but you're sure to have heard his music. He is one of the world's leading songwriters having sold in excess of eighty million records with hits such as 'Delilah', 'Love Grows (Where My Rosemary Goes)', 'The Last Waltz', 'Here It Comes Again', 'Love Is All' and 'There Goes My First Love'. Barry's compositions have been recorded by Tom Jones, Barbara Streisand, Elvis Presley, Rod Stewart, Englebert Humperdink, The Drifters and Tony Christie, to name just a few. Barry has won five Ivor Novello awards, and thirteen ASCAP and BMI Awards from the USA. What you may not know is that he comes from Lancashire.

Barry was born in Spencer Road, Wigan. His father was the editor of the *Wigan Observer*, the youngest ever editor in the country. But unfortunately, when he was called up for service in the Second World War, it was discovered that he was suffering from TB. There was no cure at that time and four years later he died. Meanwhile, Barry was sent away from home to boarding school in Prestatyn, North Wales to safeguard him from infection – but as a young child between the ages of seven and eleven it was hard for him to understand why he had been sent away, and he felt rejected.

After his father's death he moved with his mother to Blackpool where she opened a boarding house or private hotel as she preferred to call it. Here she met and married an American GI who came to stay. The marriage turned out to be not a particularly happy one, but the couple moved to the USA and, after National Service in the Royal Marines, Barry followed them.

He wanted to be a singer or an actor and hitch hiked down the famous Route 66 to Los Angeles where he failed miserably. Back in this country for a holiday he decided to have once last crack at his ambitions in London. Here he met singer Tommy Bruce, wrote a song for him called 'You're My Little Girl' and became his manager. Tommy's career did not take off, but Barry's did and along with Les Reed he wrote many of the hit songs of the 60s and 70s.

Following his successes he had what he describes as 'fallow years' where he played golf and enjoyed life. But his creative impulse to write songs never left him and he returned to show business with a company named Xenex Music Group which was set up with brothers Stuart and Ian Mack and Nick Constable to nurture new talent amongst singers, songwriters and producers. Barry now lives in a leafy suburb in Kingston-on-Thames with his Californian born wife, Elizabeth. They have a daughter Maggie and a son Tyler. Barry also has a daughter Aimi from his first marriage.

As well as continuing to write his own songs Barry now tutors a songwriting course for the Arvon Foundation and performs his one man show, *Remember Delilah*, which has raised millions of pounds for charity. He says that the first time round he did it because he needed the money. But now he says: 'I'm doing it because I love it.'

Pat Seed

1928-1984

Cancer campaigner

Pat Seed was born in Salford on St Patrick's Day, 17 March 1928. Christened Patricia Victoria she writes in her autobiography *One Day At A Time* that she was an extremely healthy child 'with more energy than most grown ups knew what to do with'.

She attended Halton Bank Junior School in Salford and then Tootal Road Secondary School from where she was evacuated to Lancaster at the outbreak of the Second World War.

By 1943 she had returned to the city and began work as a junior in the accounts department of the *Manchester Guardian and Evening News*. She had always enjoyed writing at school and this job awakened her interest in journalism, so she went on to work as a junior reporter for the *Salford City Reporter*.

When she was twenty-one years old she moved with her parents to Bilsborrow near Garstang and at the church there she met Geoffrey Seed, the eldest son of the local headmaster. She and Geoffrey married two years later on 20 October 1951. They lived at Churchtown and adopted two children: Michael and Helen. In 1961 the family moved to Garstang where Pat worked part-time as a secretary for Missions To Seamen and became the superintendent of the Sunday School at St Thomas's Church. Later she returned to journalism as a freelance news reporter for three local papers and life seemed good until, in April 1976, she was diagnosed with cancer.

Whilst being treated at the Christie Hospital in Manchester Pat was sent to the Manchester University Medical School to be scanned by their Computerised Axial Tomography X-ray Whole Body Scanner, known as a CAT or CT scanner. It was invented by Dr Godfrey Hounsfield who worked for EMI, probably better known for its music recording industry. The scanner produced a layer by layer cross section picture of the inside of the body, showing the position, shape, size, density and even chemical composition of tumours, giving a much more accurate and faster diagnosis than previously and preventing the need for exploratory surgery.

When Pat asked why the Christie Hospital didn't have a scanner of its own she was told that at a cost of half a million pounds the NHS simply couldn't afford one. And when she asked why the hospital didn't appeal for money she was told that they weren't allowed to. So

Pat began to wonder about the possibility of raising half a million pounds herself to buy a CT scanner.

When the National Health Service began in 1948 a clause was added to the Health Act that forbade hospitals appealing for funds, as the government of the day wanted to emphasise that health care was now free. When Pat began her fund raising the Christie was not even allowed to put up a small poster in the outpatients' department. So Pat contacted Walter Clegg, who was the Conservative MP for North Fylde and at the next meeting of the Standing Committee for North-West Regional Affairs on 27 April 1977, he raised the issue with Roland Moyle, the Minister for

Pat Seed

Health. In a written reply, dated 19 May, Mr Moyle agreed that the ruling was too restrictive and said that he saw no reason why 'health authorities and district management teams should not encourage local fund raising activities...'. Consequently the law was amended.

Although she had been given only around six months to live, Pat began work on her campaign. Mike Marsh at Radio Blackburn, had already made a programme called 'Cancer and Me', broadcast on 22 August 1976, based on Pat's written articles and followed by a phone-in which lasted for forty minutes. At that time cancer was not a subject that was openly discussed and later, in her autobiography, Pat writes about a talk she gave to a Women's Institute about cancer when hardly anyone turned up, as if they were afraid that she would infect them with the disease.

One of her objectives was to replace people's fear of cancer with 'positive public co-operation in the fight against the disease'. Through her contact with Mike Marsh she persuaded BBC *Look North* to make a short programme about her and her campaign, even though the total required had now risen to three quarters of a million pounds because the hospital would also need a purpose built unit to house the scanner.

After the programme was aired, donations began to arrive and an account was opened at the Garstang branch of the National Westminster Bank in the name of The Pat Seed Appeal Fund. Within a fortnight the fund had over £2,000 and people across the county began to organise charity nights, raffles, garden fetes, sponsored walks and many more events to raise money. Pat worked harder than ever before in her life, spending fifteen to sixteen hours a day answering letters, opening events and appearing on radio and television, despite her illness. But it soon became too much for her to cope with alone. The Appeal Fund was given charity status and a team of volunteers moved in to help send out 7,000 letters to firms across the north-west to appeal for money, and Pauline Heaton, wife of the Junior School headmaster, was employed as a secretary to assist her. Comedian Ken Dodd became a Patron of the Appeal, performing shows to help raise funds and by Christmas 1977 £40,000 had been raised.

The fundraising was given a huge boost by an idea suggested by Julé Hayward, a cancer patient from Burnley. She said that all it needed was a million people to give 75p each and the target would be reached. It was this idea that led to the yellow *I'm One In A Million* badges that were sold at 50p each in aid of the Appeal Fund. But Pat had been reluctant to spend cash that people had given for the scanner on the production of the badges, especially when she found that the cost would be around £20,000. However, Julé and her husband Patrick offered to use their own money and the scheme went ahead.

By its first anniversary, the Appeal Fund had over half a million pounds. Then Pat appeared on the *Russell Harty Show* wearing one of the badges and thousands of donations from all across the country were received. By Friday 28 April 1978, the Appeal Fund reached its three quarters of a million pound target. In the Queen's birthday honours list Pat was awarded the MBE and by the end of June the donations reached a million pounds with a cheque for just over £300 from Northfold County Infant School.

The foundation stone for the scanner building was laid on 22 January 1979, two years after Pat was told she had six months to live. The scanner itself arrived on 29 November that same year and the new department, named The Pat Seed Building was officially opened by HRH the Duchess of Kent on 24 April 1980. Dr Godfrey Hounsfield, the scanner's inventor, who also won a Nobel Prize for his achievements and was knighted, was also present. And Sacha Hayward, the small daughter of Julé, who had sadly died before she could see the scanner arrive, presented a bouquet of flowers to the Duchess.

But although Pat Seed worked endlessly for the benefit of others who would come after her there was no happy ending for Pat herself. Sadly, she outlived her husband Geoffrey, who she praises so much in both her books for his support and care during her illness and her fundraising. He was one of the sixteen people killed at the water pumping house at Abbeystead on Wednesday 23 May 1984, when a group of local residents were attending a presentation which had been organised to allay their anxieties about the effects of the installation on the winter flooding of the lower Wyre Valley. Shortly after a demonstration of the water pumping began there was an intense flash, followed by a severe explosion.

The loss of her husband, who had given her so much love and support over the years must have been a cruel shock to Pat and ten weeks later she herself died.

Pat's ashes together with those of her husband, Geoffrey are in the Garden of Remembrance at St Thomas' Church in Garstang. In the church there is a book of remembrance and a stand bought by Pat in memory of Geoff, but dedicated in memory of them both.

At her death the Appeal Fund had over three million pounds, but her legacy did not stop there. Her fund raising charity, The Pat Seed Appeal Fund has, to date, raised over nine million pounds and financed the installation of four CT scanners, two MRI scanners and one Linear Accelerator as well as many smaller items including lasers, ultrasound and fibre optics. March 2007 will be the thirtieth anniversary of the fund which is to pay for the installation of a PET CT scanner at a cost of £900,000. Without the fund the Christie Hospital wouldn't have been able to afford this scanner for several years, so it's fitting that Pat Seed's fund should still be providing the finance for new, vital technology.

Anyone interested in supporting The Pat Seed Appeal Fund should contact Pauline Heaton on 01995 604047 or write to her c/o the Christie Hospital.

A memorial stone and plaque was unveiled in January 2000 in Garstang by Pat's nine year old grandaughter, Emma. In the centre it reads: "The Pat Seed Memorial Garden – One Day at a Time" and around the outside it says: "Patricia Victoria Seed MBE MA 1928-1984. Cancer Campaigner"

Nick Park

1958-

Creator of Wallace and Gromit

Born Nicholas Wulstan Park in Preston on 6 December 1958, Nick Park, the son of a photographer, is the creator of Wallace & Gromit. From childhood he was a gifted artist and covered his schoolbooks with cartoons, although one teacher warned him that he would never make a living from it!

He also enjoyed writing humorous stories, and although most of us give up Plasticine® when we leave infant school, Nick continued to use it, first making films in his parents' attic and then throughout his time at Sheffield Polytechnic where he studied for a degree in Communication Arts. While at the National Film and Television School in Beaconsfield he first worked on his comedy about a man

Nick Park © 2002 Aardman Animations Ltd, by Richard Laing

and his dog, which became Wallace, now voiced by Peter Sallis, and his silent, but possibly cleverer, dog Gromit.

Nick was always fascinated by animation and says: "Plasticine was available when I was a teenager and started doing animation. I wanted to be like Disney, trying to film with plastic cels, but it was all too expensive."

Whilst studying at the National Film and Television School, Nick spent two summers working for David Sproxton and Peter Lord at Aardman in Bristol, and he joined them full time in 1985. It was here that he finished the film he had begun for his graduation: *A Grand Day Out*. The film won the BAFTA award for Best Short Animated Film in 1990 and was nominated for an Academy Award in the same year.

His second film *Creature Comforts* also received much acclaim at many major film festivals and was awarded an Oscar® for the Best Short Animated Film of 1990. It was also the inspiration for a series of adverts promoting electric heating, and these brought Nick's creations to the notice of a much wider public. *Creature Comforts* was later revived as a television series in 2003.

In 1993 Aardman produced Nick's second Wallace & Gromit film *The Wrong Trousers*. The comedy thriller, lasting thirty minutes, was first shown by BBC television on Boxing Day that year and it became one of the most successful short animated films ever made, winning over forty top awards including an Oscar® for Best Short Animated Film from the Academy of Motion Picture Arts and Sciences in March 1994.

His next film, *Wallace & Gromit: A Close Shave*, also shown by the BBC on Christmas Eve in 1995, brought Nick Park a third Oscar®. He also made front page news when he went to New York for a promotional tour of the film and left the original motorbike and sidecar with Wallace and Gromit in the back of a cab. Following an appeal the cab driver read about it in the *New York Post*, checked his cab and returned them. He was offered a reward of $500, but refused to take it.

On 30 October 1996 Nick Park was awarded an honorary Doctor of Arts degree by Bath University. The following year on 25 November 1997 he was awarded the CBE for services to the Animated Film Industry.

In 2000 the first feature-length Aardman animation *Chicken Run* became one of the most successful British films ever made. Nick Park co-directed it with Peter Lord and actor Mel Gibson was the voice of the rooster.

Following these successes, the American film company Dreamworks, owned by Steven Spielberg, offered to bring Wallace and Gromit to the big screen. The result was *Wallace & Gromit: The Curse of the Were-Rabbit*, released in 2005 and named as Outstanding British Film of the Year at the BAFTA awards in 2006, the first time an animation has won this award. It also went on to win Nick a fourth Oscar®.

Once again the film doesn't rely on modern computer graphics but is made frame by frame, minutely manipulating the Plasticine figures between each shot. It's a time-consuming job, but one which results in very human facial expressions and characteristics. There are 115,000 frames of finished footage in the film, and it took five years to complete. With thirty animators, around two minutes are completed each week.

But it is not just the technology that makes Nick's creations so popular, it's the personalities and the stories that he creates. Although they are cartoons and children do enjoy them they are just as popular, if not more popular, with adults – and much of the humour is aimed at adults. In *The Curse of the Were-Rabbit* for example there are many references to other films. "The inspiration for the story was some of the classic horror movies," said Nick Park, though this one is about prize vegetables rather than blood.

Nick Park continues to work on animations for Aardman. He says: "My animation has developed over the years but my fascination for the magic of animation which began at thirteen has remained unchanged."

Wayne Hemingway

1961-

From 'Red or Dead' to affordable housing

Wayne Hemingway was born in Morecambe in 1961. His father is a Mohawk Indian chief named Billy Two Rivers who was a heavyweight wrestling champion when Wayne was born.

Wayne's introduction to fashion came early when his mother would dress him up as a Beatle or Elvis and parade him up and down Morecambe pier, and he says that his mother's taste was a massive influence on him.

Later, they moved to Blackburn and Wayne gained an assisted place at Queen Elizabeth's Grammar School where he gained 10 O-levels and 4 A-levels before studying for a degree in Geography and Town Planning at University College, London. When he left for London his girlfriend Gerardine went with him. Gerardine was born in Padiham in 1961 and the couple met in the Angels Disco in Burnley.

Having been interested in music from an early age, Wayne was playing in a band in London and desperately needed money to buy some equipment so he and Gerardine cleared all their unwanted clothes from their wardrobes and took them to Camden Market. Having paid £6 to rent a stall and taken £80 for the clothing they quickly realised that there was money to be made from fashion and they began Red or Dead, a fashion label that went on to win the British Fashion Council's Streetstyle Designer of the Year Award in three consecutive years from 1996 to 1998.

After twenty-one successful seasons, Wayne and Gerardine sold Red or Dead in a multi-million pound cash sale. Then, combining his design skills with his early interest in town planning Wayne, with Gerardine, set up Hemingway Design, and after criticising modern housing developments became involved with the design of houses at Gateshead on Tyneside for George Wimpey Homes that were both affordable and socially progressive.

Wayne believes that the houses where people live hugely affect their quality of life. He says, "Gardens or access to some form of secure private or semi private space is important to our well-being, we care about light and window size; porches and defensible space mean a lot to us and a richness of detail makes us feel good." The

Wayne and Gerardine Hemingway

houses at Staiths South Bank all have small gardens and are set around small green areas where children can play and residents can sit and chat. Cars are not given priority and have to be parked around the back.

This project was followed by work in Manchester for the regeneration of afford-able apartments in the Northern Quarter, The Birchin. Hemingway Design has also worked with West Lancashire Council and English Partnerships on a project to create a new look for the 1960s-purpose-built town of Skelmersdale; on a plan for Whitehaven in Cumbria, which suffered huge job losses after the decommis-sioning of the Sellafield Nuclear Power Plant; and with Gateshead, Newcastle and Blackburn councils on regeneration projects.

Wayne is interested in many forms of art and his 'coffee table' book on art called *Just Above the Mantelpiece*, published by Booth Clibborn Editions in 2000 celebrates his art collection of paintings that he inherited from his grandmother, which were mostly bought from mail order catalogues. The images of white horses galloping through the surf, little boys with huge eyes and dusky native girls are familiar to most people and thought to be poor taste by many, but Wayne rejects this viewpoint and believes that they are examples of collectable pop art.

He also writes for architectural and housing publications and is a public speaker. He is a Professor in the Development and Planning Department of Northumbria University, and has judged many international design competitions including the Stirling Prize and the regeneration of Byker in Newcastle and Salford in Greater Manchester. He has also been awarded a doctorate in design from Wolverhampton University and an MBA in Fashion from Surrey.

He is the chairman of Building For Life and a member of the judging panel that gives awards to house builders for their developments. Building For Life has over twenty criteria that it uses to judge a successful housing development including the character of the area, features that give it a community feel, a layout that promotes use by people rather than cars, features that reduce its environmental impact, as well as sustainability and a range of accommodation for all sorts of people.

Wayne and Gerardine run their design and consultancy business from a house in Wembley that used to be their family home, but they now live in West Sussex, near the coast. Wayne, a keen family man, with four children says he is looking forward to becoming a grandfather and although he made his name in the fashion industry, Wayne enjoys his own unique style saying that he wears 'pensioner chic', consisting of brown slacks, sensible shoes and occasionally, a cardigan; and much of what he wears consists of second-hand bargains. But although his name will be forever linked with fashion it is his campaigning for better housing which will probably have the most impact on other people's lives.

People Index

Places Index